# NLP

Utilize Natural Language Processing To Cultivate The Identical Psychology And Aptitudes Demonstrated By Exemplary Leaders, Resulting In Enhanced Decision-Making Abilities And A Defined Vision

**Jared Bradshaw**

# TABLE OF CONTENT

The Realms Of Thought Within Our Cognitive Faculty............1

Emphatic People............32

The Mechanisms, Locations, And Rationale Behind The Efficacy Of Neuro Linguistic Programming............56

Types Of Narcissism............79

Attract More Wealth............89

Effective Natural Language Processing Techniques With The Potential To Transform Your Life............106

Attain Success By Utilizing NLP Modeling............117

Blackpool Rock............144

Case Studies............155

# The Realms Of Thought Within Our Cognitive Faculty.

Perhaps you possess knowledge of distinguishing between what is genuine and what is not. Consider the following: you possess a twin sibling with whom you cohabit in an identical living space. It might be tempting to assume that the environment encompassing both of you is homogeneous, yet I regret to inform you that this is not the case.

From the moment of our birth, our observations commence, initiating a phase marked by an initial state of disorder, wherein the influx of incomprehensible information inundates our consciousness. An overwhelming plethora of visual stimuli, auditory input, olfactory impressions, gustatory experiences, and physical sensations inundates our senses. The cognitive faculties commence the process of organizing all elements, employing linguistic systems as their sole means of thought, which predominantly relies on utilizing imagery, sounds, flavors, sensations, and scents. They serve as fundamental building blocks within the intellectual realm.

The reality in which you perceive and experience exists solely within the confines of your consciousness, and is not shared by any other individual. One's cognitive processes shape the reality they inhabit, the interpersonal bonds they form, their behavior towards others, their self-perception, and the perceptual frameworks they construct.

The human brain possesses various sensory faculties such as visual perception, auditory perception, somatic sensations, gustatory sensations, and olfactory sensations, albeit with distinct levels of utilization and intensity.

Subsequently, you will gain enhanced comprehension of the subject matter at hand.

What is the nature of your introspective experience?

Observe the garments you are adorned in, the style with which you have donned them, and the manner in which you have retrieved them from the wardrobe. In essence, the entire procedure culminates in its eventual implementation. Now contemplate the garments you adorned in the previous day, employing this technique to retrieve the aforementioned information, thereby enabling you to reminisce the sensations and experiences associated with wearing said attire. The mental faculties created that visual representation for you.

It is imperative to acknowledge that the perception of an image may not be aligned with that of the previous day, as it is inevitably influenced by the diverse range of emotions experienced in each individual circumstance. It is imperative that a door is present at the entrance of a dwelling. Having read this, it is likely that the notion of the door immediately comes to mind. Given your familiarity with the location, envision that door in great detail. Once you have it in your thoughts, proceed to open it, and you will be greeted by the distinctive sound that accompanies its unveiling. Experience the strength that is exerted upon opening it, whether it is delicate like a gentle gust or substantial due to its contact with the ground.

Carefully contemplate every aspect of this situation, including each sensation and the information that you have absorbed unconsciously. You will observe that there is an extensive amount of data stored.

Consider the majestic mountains, envision yourself amidst a vast expanse of greenery, reclining on your back with your elbow making contact with the moistened soil. If you are predominantly right-handed, conceptualize the scenario in which your left elbow is the point of emphasis, and vice versa. Subsequently, endeavor to execute a scratching movement using the aforementioned elbow, which possesses a lesser degree of proficiency. Attempt to create the initial letter representation of your name. In order to accomplish this task, you must engage in the imaginative exercise of envisioning the specific letter that corresponds to the initial of your given name. As you perused the text, you undoubtedly noticed the letter conspicuously imprinted upon the ground, undoubtedly perceiving the evidence of the grass's impairment by your aforementioned actions. Prior to these events, you initially visualized the lyrics in your mind.

May I inquire about your perspective on this correspondence? Certain individuals may perceive it in written form, while others may observe it as a luminous signage, a large outdoor advertisement, or an ornate letter in a Gothic style. Your cognition perceived all of these aspects, including the intricacies of generating written language using your non-dominant elbow.

Consider alternative entrances, ponder the seaside, reflect upon mundane locations in your routine, contemplate the distinct odors that accompany doors when they are opened, and meditate on the sounds that greet you upon entering your residence or place of employment. When considering each of these, one experiences varied emotions, such as the scent emanating from the door adjacent to the dentist's office, which invokes fear, or the fragrance of newly spritzed cologne as one enters the doorway leading to the beloved's bedside. , in which you experience joy and satisfaction. Every site elicits various emotions, including pleasant, unpleasant, and often neutral. These sensations encompass a multitude of stimuli that permeate into the depths of your cognition, imparting copious amounts of information.

The brain possesses the capacity to categorize and store all of this information. It retains all cognitive, perceptual, emotional, auditory, and imaginative experiences.

Submodality

"The model of submodalities is, without a doubt, one of the most noteworthy contributions I have made to date." ~ Richard Bandler, Co-Creator of NLP

If limited to acquiring one NLP technique, I highly recommend prioritizing the study of Submodality. The majority of NLP techniques draw heavily from the principles and concepts inherent to submodality. Furthermore, a comprehensive grasp of submodality could empower one to develop original techniques tailored to their unique needs and preferences.

So what is submodality? First, let us delve into the topic of the Representational System.

We acquire data from the external environment by means of our five senses. The human faculties employed in perceiving or apprehending stimuli can be categorized as visual perception, auditory perception, tactile perception, olfactory perception, and gustatory perception. In the context of NLP , it is referred to as the Visual (V), Auditory (A), Kinesthetic (K), Olfactory (O), and Gustatory (G) modalities, commonly denoted as VAKOG. They are representational system.

In the realm of existence, among the five aforementioned representational systems, it is noteworthy that only three hold prominence, namely visual (V), auditory (A), and kinesthetic (K). Given their infrequent usage, O and G have been classified within the K category.

When engaging with the external environment, the brain gathers, apprehends, or documents the information utilizing a system of representation. Your visual senses perceive the image, auditory senses detect the sound, and tactile senses experience the touch or sensation.

Subsequently, the brain shall proceed to selectively process the information. The cognitive mechanism that operates inherently is commonly referred to as the Meta Model. The meta model encompasses the processes of generalization, deletion, and distortion. Due to the meta model, we engage in the process of encoding and retaining information within our brain in a specific manner.

Let us now proceed to our discussion on the topic of submodality. Submodality refers to the manner in which we delineate, encode, or construct the framework of our internalized perceptions. Submodalities refer to the characteristics inherent in our system of representation. Vision encompasses features such as shape, hue, spatial arrangement, measurements, magnitude, and the like. The auditory experience encompasses elements such as tempo, stereo/mono configuration, duration, and various others. Kinesthetic encompasses factors such as spatial orientation, temperature perception, tactile qualities, and level of stimulation.

I will provide an explanatory example in order to facilitate your comprehension of the concepts pertaining to representational system, meta model, and submodalities. Capture an image of a specific landscape utilizing a single lens reflex (SLR) camera, with deliberate emphasis on a particular aspect. The camera serves as a visual depiction. The image acquired from the camera is referred to as visual modality.

The photograph presents a dissimilar depiction when compared to the physical landscape. The picture exhibits numerous alterations. Certain portions have been removed due to the inherent limitations of capturing the entirety of objects within a single photographic frame. Certain portions have undergone distortion, resulting in a blurring and lack of clarity. Additionally, one may observe certain general patterns where particular colors prevail in certain sections.

As a consequence of the selective use of focus in capturing the photograph, certain elements exhibit characteristics such as blurriness, a partially obscured darkness, monochromatic contrast, varying degrees of brightness and darkness, an expansive range, and other similar attributes. Those are submodalities. Upon viewing the photograph, one is likely to form a distinct impression, such as, "Oh, it is truly stunning," or "It appears to have been captured by a skilled photographer."

Nevertheless, should you opt to capture an image of identical surroundings with altered emphasis and representation, a distinct perception shall arise, despite the fact that it constitutes a depiction of the aforementioned scenery.

When we undergo an occurrence, our brain will perceive it through the utilization of our sensory faculties. Subsequently, our cognitive filter will selectively process the information acquired from the occasion in accordance with our established beliefs. The information, which has been generalized, omitted, and altered, is subsequently stored within our brain utilizing distinct codes known as submodalities.

What is the distinguishing feature or unique characteristic of this submodality? EXCEPTIONALLY SIGNIFICANT! By altering the submodalities of the encounter, we have the capacity to modify the outcomes of the experience. All events are inherently neutral; however, it is the submodalities of one's internal representation, specifically how the event is mentally constructed, that attribute qualities such as negativity-positivity, sadness-joy, fear-exhilaration, and so forth to the event.

An individual who was deeply enamored, during moments of envisioning their beloved's countenance, perceived distinct submodalities. For instance, the visage was typically luminous, animated, vibrant, evoking a sense of joy and similar sentiments.

Nevertheless, at some point he discovered that his beloved had been engaging in infidelity. Upon attempting to conjure an image of his beloved once more, the submodalities underwent a change: the visual depiction shifted towards the left, the hues lost their vibrancy, and a sense of anguish enveloped him.

Additionally, once he had successfully managed to erase all memory of his beloved, it became apparent that the submodalities had undergone a remarkable transformation. The image transitioned into a monochromatic palette, distant in perspective, devoid of movement, and exuding a sense of chilliness.

This invention is indeed remarkable. The developers of NLP conducted diligent research on it, ultimately arriving at the finding that deliberate alteration or adjustment of the submodalities results in a corresponding alteration of the event's significance, consequently impacting our emotions and sentiments.

Through the utilization of submodalities, it is possible to diminish the magnitude of our emotional experiences, thereby effectively mitigating emotions such as trauma, guilt, resentment, and hate. The utilization of submodalities also permits us to amplify the magnitude of emotions we desire to experience, such as augmenting sensations of love, happiness, confidence, and so forth.

On the Internet
Individuals who exhibit traits of dark personalities have been observed to engage in online trolling behavior. Consequently, they exhibit indications of sadism, Machiavellianism, psychopathy,

and antisocial conduct. Cyberbullying entails the conscious and persistent act of engaging in bullying behavior towards an individual through digital platforms. The ordeal can be distressing and emotionally unsettling, particularly due to its typical anonymity. This modus operandi has emerged as a prevailing preference among a considerable number of individuals in contemporary times, with the involvement of even the younger generation in participating in cyberbullying activities that perpetuate threats and demean others. "The strategies employed for cyberbullying encompass:

Sharing digitally mutable photos on online platforms, particularly in the context of deteriorating relationships.
Developing digital platforms for the purpose of engaging in contentious and antagonistic exchanges characterized by

bashful and malicious rhetoric among multiple participants, resulting in recipients being inundated with a continuous stream of hurtful messages on a daily basis, thereby subjecting these individuals to profound detrimental psychological impacts.

The effectiveness of cyber-bullying on the victim is magnified by the common occurrence of anonymity, as the identities of the perpetrators are typically concealed, setting it apart from conventional forms of bullying. This form of assault is commonly referred to as covert hostility. Individuals exhibiting traits associated with a darker personality gravitate towards this platform due to their heightened comfort in expressing themselves towards others online compared to offline interactions. In the conventional context, it becomes evident that the instances of bullying were premeditated and deliberate. The primary motive behind their participation in such activities can potentially encompass the desire for retribution and the intention to subdue their victims when met with resistance. Given that this method of assault lacks a confrontational nature, the perpetrators may express a predilection for it due to its capacity to afford them a sensation of safety in maintaining their anonymity. Psychopathy demonstrates the highest degree of correlation with both forms of bullying, succeeded by Machiavellianism and subsequently bullying.

Addressing the Presence of the Dark Triad in the Workplace

In conclusion, we will elucidate several strategies that can be employed to effectively manage individuals possessing dark triad personality traits in a professional setting. If there happens to be an individual characterized by narcissistic, Machiavellian, or psychopathic tendencies within your professional environment, please proceed with the following information:

Narcissists

It has been previously determined that individuals with narcissistic tendencies can lead to challenges within the professional environment. Arguably, the most unfortunate aspect is the lack of control over the settings themselves. You must make necessary modifications to accommodate them. In order to ascertain the viability of these measures, it is imperative to examine the organization and verify that promotion and compensation are not granted to individuals who exhibit narcissistic traits. Should the organization, in any capacity, promote or endorse such inclinations, it may become necessary for you to seek alternate professional opportunities. If that is not the case, please proceed with the following instructions:

Please ensure that all pertinent information is documented. In the event that verbal instructions are communicated in your workplace, you have the option to submit a formal request for these directives to be transmitted to you via email instead. In such manner, you will possess a written record of the narcissist's words and corresponding timeframe. An alternative formulation in a formal tone could be as follows: "In addition, it is advisable to document their statements and subsequently engage in a detailed review together in order to ensure the utmost precision during the review process."

✓ Given this particular personality trait, you fully adhere to a proactive approach where no room is left for uncertainty. Record occurrences, schedules, calendar dates, and exact quotations as they could prove advantageous in the future, particularly if the need to seek legal counsel arises.

✓ Employing avoidance is another strategy one can employ when navigating interactions with narcissistic individuals. Being an individual with traits from the dark triad, they consistently seek opportunities to undermine you within the professional environment. It is imperative that you refrain from providing them with any opportunities whatsoever, as they will exert every effort to discover your vulnerabilities and manipulate them. Their deceitful tactics might encompass, for instance, exploiting your familial ties in order to undermine you, through disparaging remarks made in moments of strained interpersonal relationships. The remarks made in this instance could potentially imply, for instance, that you do not exhibit exemplary mothering abilities, particularly if your colleagues are aware of your prioritization of familial responsibilities. Typically, in the event that a remark of this nature arises, it typically lacks relevance to the current circumstances. It is important to discern that this behavior is characteristic of a classic narcissist, attempting to engage you in a power play wherein they will ultimately exert control over the outcome. They comprehend that exploiting your position within the family would serve as the optimal strategy to undermine your integrity. In the event that this occurs, refrain from participating in a dialogue with them. Please bear in mind that this is the inherent personality of the narcissist, and it is unrelated to your own circumstances or actions. In spite of all the enticement to retaliate, exercise restraint, and depart without uttering a single syllable. This will not simply create a sense of curiosity about your perspectives, but rather instill a profound sense of doubt about their own capacity to assert authority over various circumstances. As previously mentioned, it is essential to record all pertinent information in situations of this nature, including but not limited to dates, location, and direct quotations.

Furthermore, it is essential to acknowledge the deliberate nature behind a narcissist's selection of you as their target, while understanding that the entire situation is not driven by personal motives. Typically, in situations involving a narcissist as the aggressor, it is not due to any wrongdoing on your part but rather your perceived superiority in certain aspects. Indeed, it should be noted that the narcissist harbors a significant aversion towards individuals who are perceived to have achieved greater success or prosperity than themselves. Consequently, they will purposefully target you, not due to any transgressions on your part, but as a result of their own profound inner feelings of insecurity. It can be perplexing for individuals who become entangled with narcissists in a professional setting, as these individuals often consistently display an appearance of having everything well-organized. Upon the realization that their conflicts are not of a personal nature, one becomes aware that disengaging from a narcissistic individual is not only a simpler course of action, but also a viable and gratifying alternative to engaging with them.

✓ Minimize the sharing of personal information or opinions with the workplace narcissist to reduce vulnerability to their criticism. It is crucial for you to comprehend that individuals with narcissistic tendencies possess a remarkable aptitude for actively seeking and soliciting the viewpoints of others. And as soon as you avert your gaze, the narcissist will mercilessly impale you with the most innocuous of viewpoints. For example, when he inquires about your opinion on a team consisting of four members, you could express that you believe the team is commendable, although Sally's skills could have been put to good use on Reinhardt's team. In light of this routine observation, it is worth noting that the narcissist may deliberately choose a moment when your relationship with Sally is strained to strategically reveal this information, with the intention of creating division and asserting dominance. He may assert that you mentioned Sally's inadequacy for her team. Narcissists employ this strategy as a means of survival, distorting the statements of others. Hence, it is incumbent upon you to discern the manipulative tactic employed by the narcissist and to abstain from interacting with him. When faced with inquiries regarding personal viewpoints, it is advisable to redirect the conversation by engaging in actions like physically distancing oneself or gracefully transitioning to a different topic. Under any circumstances, it is crucial not to provide the narcissist with an opportunity for manipulation or exploitation.

It is not out of the ordinary to encounter the workplace narcissist approaching you with requests for a private meeting. In the event that this occurs, it is advisable to bring along another individual to serve as your observer. Utilizing a witness confers two distinct advantages upon you. Firstly, the presence of a witness has the potential to dissuade a narcissist from uttering remarks that they are aware may incite disorder. Secondly, in the event that the narcissist were to fabricate falsehoods in the future regarding your encounter, the witness can subsequently provide testimony in your support by virtue of having observed the unfolding of said events.

✓ To flourish in an organization where a narcissist is present, it is advisable to limit interactions. This guidance may appear straightforward, yet adhering to it can prove to be one of the most challenging tasks. Nevertheless, every cloud has a silver lining. One positive aspect of this situation is that this strategy tends to yield positive results on almost all occasions. Narcissists become anxious when you refuse to engage in their manipulative tactics and opt for an alternative approach instead. If you find yourself in close proximity to the narcissist due to sharing the same professional setting, it is advisable to restrict your exchanges solely to essential information. As delineated previously, refrain from succumbing to the temptation of expressing personal viewpoints. If you find it untenable to continue working with the narcissist in close proximity within the building, you have the option to facilitate and formally seek a reassignment to another position within the same premises.

✓ It is crucial to ensure a comprehensive understanding of your legal rights. It is imperative for one to comprehend that individuals afflicted with narcissism possess a shrewd character. You will observe that the individual exhibiting narcissistic tendencies will strategically provoke your emotional triggers, causing slight irritation without directly engaging in any illicit conduct. As a result, they possess comprehension of their actions. Nevertheless, as a result of their inherent propensity for self-indulgence, they frequently transgress boundaries, and ultimately, they overstep societal norms. It is crucial to comprehend the extent of one's responsibilities and entitlements within an organization, particularly when dealing with a manager who exhibits narcissistic tendencies. The United States' Equal Employment Opportunity Commission, as an illustration, asserts that individuals should not be subject to disparate treatment or discriminatory practices on the grounds of their gender, age, nationality, or creed. Additionally, it is the employer's responsibility to ensure that the employees are working in an environment that is conducive to their well-being, to prevent them from being placed in an intolerable situation where their ability to thrive is compromised. In addition to addressing discriminatory practices, the legal framework provides protection against both harassment and retaliation when individuals exercise their right to report such conduct by their employers. Hence, the responsibility falls upon you to determine to what extent you wish to build a case against your narcissistic supervisor in the workplace.

# Emphatic People

Individuals with a proclivity towards emphasis demonstrate resemblances to those who exhibit high sensitivity; however, diverging from the latter, they possess a heightened awareness of the emotions of others and the prevailing aura of the surrounding environment. They have a propensity to internalize the suffering of others to such an extent that it becomes ingrained within their own being. Indeed, for certain individuals, discerning between another person's discomfort and their own can pose a challenge. Individuals with a strong capacity for empathy make for ideal partners, as they possess the ability to deeply sense and understand the emotions experienced by others. Nevertheless, this renders them remarkably susceptible to manipulation, thereby attracting the attention of unscrupulous individuals.

Individuals with ill intent possess the ability to simulate particular emotions and effectively communicate these emotions to individuals who are empathetic, subsequently causing these individuals to experience these emotions as genuine. That renders them vulnerable to exploitation. Individuals who possess an inclination towards strong displays of emotion become prime targets for manipulative individuals with psychopathic tendencies, as they are highly attuned to empathizing with others. A fraudulent individual has the ability to fabricate narratives surrounding financial hardships, thereby deceiving sympathetic individuals and fraudulently amassing substantial amounts of money.

One potential alternative in a formal tone could be: "The challenge inherent in being emphatic is that due to the intensity of one's emotions, there is a tendency to overlook doubts regarding individuals, as the inclination is to extend assistance to an individual who may ultimately be deceptive rather than withhold aid from an individual telling the truth."

Individuals with a heightened display of empathy possess magnanimous qualities and exhibit a propensity towards remarkable generosity, frequently at their own expense. They possess a profound sense of altruism, experiencing remorse when witnessing the sufferings of those in their vicinity, even in situations beyond their control and influence. Individuals with ill intentions find it effortless to manipulate susceptible individuals into experiencing feelings of guilt. They exhibit the generous nature of individuals who would willingly surrender their entire life savings in order to aid their friends in alleviating their financial burden, even at the expense of their own financial ruin.

Individuals with ill intent often gravitate towards individuals who possess a strong capacity for empathy, as they are more susceptible to exploitation. Individuals with a proclivity for intensity tend to proactively evade engaging in close interpersonal connections due to their awareness of the ease with which they become fully immersed in such relationships, potentially jeopardizing their sense of self in the course of doing so. Nevertheless, manipulators will persistently pursue individuals who possess strong empathy, as they are aware that they can easily manipulate them into fulfilling their desires once they have gained their guilt.

Dread of Solitude

A considerable number of individuals harbor apprehension towards solitude, albeit this fear is particularly intensified among a minority fraction of the populace. This particular type of fear can induce a profound state of paralysis in individuals who undergo such an experience, rendering them susceptible to manipulation by malicious individuals. As an illustration, a considerable number of individuals persist within dysfunctional relationships due to apprehensions regarding their incapacity to discover alternative companions who will reciprocate their affection, should they choose to terminate their ties with an abusive partner. Manipulators possess the ability to discern this fear within the victim, and they will frequently exert all possible efforts to intensify it in order to ensure the individual is incapacitated by it. Individuals who harbor apprehensions pertaining to solitude have the capacity to endure or justify various forms of mistreatment.

The apprehension of solitude is readily discernible in a prospective target. Individuals who exhibit this type of fear often display a noticeable degree of anxiety during the initial stages of relationships, occasionally appearing overly dependent or clingy. Whereas individuals in the general population may perceive clinginess as a warning sign, manipulative individuals recognize it as a favorable occasion to take advantage of others. If one develops an emotional bond with them, they will employ manipulative tactics to further reinforce one's reliance upon them. The manipulator possesses the ability to deprive the victim of love and affection, such as employing the tactic of the silent treatment. This leads the victim to apprehensively anticipate rejection, prompting them to act out of a sense of desperation and surrender further control to the manipulator.

The apprehension towards solitude is largely constructed by society and has a greater impact on women in comparison to men. Throughout multiple generations, our society has instilled the belief in women that their ultimate purpose in life is to enter into matrimony and start a family. As a result, even those women who identify as progressive and reject this societal construct find themselves burdened by the persistent social expectations to conform to these outdated norms. However, it should be acknowledged that males similarly experience apprehension towards solitude.

Individuals who possess unresolved feelings of abandonment originating from their early developmental years often confront heightened levels of apprehension and distress regarding the state of solitude. Additionally, there exist individuals who may not inherently experience apprehension towards solitude as a whole; nevertheless, they harbor anxieties about becoming disconnected from the significant individuals in their existence. As an illustration, numerous individuals find themselves in abusive or dysfunctional relationships due to their fear of undergoing separation from their children.

Apprehension of Letting Others Down

We all experience a certain degree of duty towards the individuals in our lives; however, certain individuals harbor an intense apprehension of failing to meet the expectations of others. This form of trepidation resembles the trepidation stemming from social embarrassment and social rejection, as it signifies an individual's significant regard for the perception they elicit from others. The apprehension of falling short of expectations in others can manifest organically, and it can indeed serve a purpos In this particular instance, the apprehension is indeed productive. Nevertheless, it becomes detrimental when it is targeted towards individuals who should not be subjected to it or when it necessitates sacrificing one's own well-being and contentment.

When individuals with manipulative tendencies become aware of your apprehension towards causing disappointment to others, they will seek to place you in a predicament that elicits a sense of indebtedness towards them. They will provide certain services to you, and subsequently employ manipulation techniques to foster a perception of indebtedness. They will subsequently employ manipulative tactics to induce your compliance whenever they have a favor to ask of you.

## V - Anticipating the Future

Establishing objectives and attaining them are distinct endeavors, and a significant aspect of the difficulty lies in our aptitude to thoroughly strategize for the journey towards accomplishment. Another aspect of the challenge lies in equipping ourselves with the characteristics and attributes necessary to accomplish the objectives we have established for ourselves. Many accomplished individuals affirm that the most gratifying aspect of striving towards your objectives is observing the transformation and growth of one's character throughout the process. It is highly logical to place significant importance on adequately preparing oneself to undergo such a transformation and ensuring a sense of readiness for its implementation when the time comes.

When we establish grandiose, ambitious objectives, it is effortless to contemplate the challenges that lie ahead. "We may become preoccupied with envisioning an undesirable situation:

That task will present a significant challenge to complete in written form.

Engaging in an uninterrupted six-month exercise regimen seems highly challenging.

The timeline for this project is causing considerable frustration.

Moreover, it is often simpler to overlook the importance of providing meticulous details about those difficulties and engaging in mental preparation to effectively conquer them. Furthermore, we frequently neglect to adequately equip ourselves for unforeseen circumstances that may arise during the course of our journey. Nonetheless, analogous to an athlete diligently practicing their technique countless times in anticipation of a momentous championship game, we can employ the principles of neurolinguistic programming to equip ourselves with the necessary tools to triumphantly navigate the journey towards our most audacious aspirations.

Extensive research has consistently demonstrated that when an athlete observes another athlete executing a particular movement, there is a neural response wherein electrical impulses are generated in the muscles of the observer, mimicking the same activation that would occur if the observer were physically enacting the observed movement. In a similar vein, when an athlete envisions executing the motion, genuine impulses are elicited. Remember the mirror neurons? Indeed, they are currently in operation, and we can manipulate them to our benefit. In a manner akin to how an athlete envisions their optimal performance in order to enhance the likelihood of triumph, we too have the ability to engage in such a practice.

To begin with, it is imperative that we foster the anticipation of a favorable encounter throughout our endeavors. This can be achieved through methods such as the utilization of affirmations, the practice of journaling, or the act of visualizing mentally. Utilizing a combination of various methodologies yields enhanced outcomes.

Irrespective of the approach employed, the objective remains to establish a standard of achievement, pleasure, and satisfaction in the pursuit of any endeavor we undertake. Fluent utilization of language and effective management of emotions are of utmost importance and must be tactfully harnessed to yield favorable outcomes. For instance, when formulating affirmations, it is essential to employ potent resources within our reach, such as the terms "effortlessly" and "conveniently." By utilizing these expressions, we can highlight a favorable encounter. I am confident that I will achieve a position within the top 10% of my company's global stack rankings for this quarter. I am confident that I will be able to shed ten pounds within the upcoming three months with relative ease.

Commencing with a predetermined vision and adopting an optimistic perspective significantly impacts the creation of a poised mindset capable of persevering until the very end. When constructing mental imagery of success, place emphasis on profound emotions of joy, accomplishment, and contentment. Allow these emotions to serve as your guiding beacon, leading you towards the ultimate reward awaiting you at the culmination of your voyage.

This initial stage holds immense significance in establishing the groundwork for achievement. However, subsequent to the establishment of the foundation, it is imperative that we ascertain the means by which we will attain this objective. There exists a serpentine path of obstacles and upheaval stretching between Point A and Point B. There is no cause for alarm or any compromise to our chances of success, provided that we adequately prepare for these situations, much like how athletes rehearse rigorous training exercises to face formidable competitors. Nonetheless, neglecting to strategize for and practice handling these obstacles is akin to presuming that you will be the sole candidate vying for a promotion. It can be likened to intending to be the sole team present on the football field. It is positioning oneself for inevitable failure.

When individuals terminate their pursuit of their objectives, it is typically due to insufficient readiness to undertake the journey towards their desired outcome. A diligent student who aspires to excel academically by attaining a perfect 4.0 grade point average may face the risk of near-failure upon receiving a substantial initial assignment, thereby succumbing to the overwhelming burden of increasing responsibilities. Why? Due to the fact that he solely practiced for the singular assignment outlined in his academic record, rather than devoting sixteen weeks to consistent class attendance, organizing group study sessions, and composing papers during the late hours of the night. The challenges arrived unexpectedly, and his level of preparedness proved insufficient to cope with them adequately.

Conversely, a manager who is about to undergo an interview for a role in the executive level of her organization may commence by visualizing her presence at the desk adorned with a rich maple finish situated within her future spacious office. Additionally, she has foreseen the extensive rehearsal time required over the course of the following month in order to meticulously prepare her presentation for the Board. She has envisaged her heart palpitate rapidly as she assumes her position in the interview chamber. She has envisaged the profound serenity that envelops her upon exchanging greetings with the interviewers and becoming settled. She has imagined a scenario where the interviewers pose a question for which she is unprepared, and in this situation, she graciously acknowledges their inquiry as a means of gaining time to gather her thoughts. Additionally, she carefully formulates her response and delivers a confident and coherent answer. She has imagined the challenging period following the interview, during which she experiences subtle feelings of uncertainty and unease. The Chairman herself sending her an offer letter is a scene she has imagined, eagerly anticipating the moment she opens her inbox on a Tuesday morning.

There exists a distinct disparity in the manner in which these two individuals undertook their preparation to attain their lofty objectives. The student neglected to anticipate the procedural aspects and the anticipated difficulties in advance, and when they arose, he had not prepared himself to address them. However, the manager had already anticipated the uneasiness associated with participating in the meeting and the prospect of being posed with a question to which she had not adequately prepared. In the occurrence of such events, neither perplexity nor anxiety was evident. She had mentally envisioned herself being there, and felt adequately equipped to manage the situation.

Our mirror neurons provide us with a potent mechanism to utilize neurolinguistic programming and practice for demanding circumstances. In numerous instances, it is conceivable to anticipate the emergence of specific circumstances throughout the course of action, enabling us to adequately equip ourselves to efficiently manage such eventualities. Of utmost significance, we can conceive of cultivating the appropriate mindset precisely when it is most essential. With the aid of our creative thinking and NLP techniques, we can effectively equip ourselves for precisely such occasions.

What about the instances that are beyond our ability to anticipate? It can be assumed by any rational individual that in pursuit of a specific goal, unforeseen obstacles may arise which were not initially taken into consideration. It constitutes the rationale behind incorporating additional time cushions within project schedules, allocating surplus funds in the budget, and ensuring that our vehicles never reach the point of pushing their fuel levels to the limit. Nevertheless, we can equip ourselves for such circumstances through the utilization of NLP as well. The difficulty lies in directing our mindset and honing our response in situations where a specific set of well-defined parameters is absent.

What is our envisaged approach to this matter? Merely engage in the act of allowing oneself to be taken by surprise, while maintaining utmost composure. We can leverage our prior experiences to devise situations wherein we were unexpectedly ensnared. In previous instances, our responses may have lacked composure, thereby leading to impulsive decision-making. Nevertheless, as we anticipate the forthcoming events, it would be prudent to envision responding with composure and reason, refraining from yielding to impulsive inclinations and instead thoroughly considering the situation taking into account all the available information at our disposal. Through the utilization of NLP techniques, we harness the power to train a distinct response to instances of uncertainty. Consequently, this response will inevitably manifest itself when we encounter obstacles and setbacks in our pursuit of achieving desired objectives.

Similar to how we conducted belief setting, it is imperative to execute an ecologically conscious assessment when engaging in future pacing. In order for our preparation to be effective, it is imperative that it conforms with our present or future identity. It is imperative that we maintain honesty regarding our values, beliefs, inclinations, and aspirations. It is imperative that we exercise self-reflection and maintain a realistic outlook on anticipated difficulties, as well as consider our potential initial response to these challenges.

It is of utmost importance to refrain from deceiving ourselves in these matters, as doing so will only undermine the effectiveness of our preparation. If we possess self-awareness regarding our tendencies towards anxiety and impulsive behavior, it is inappropriate to entertain the notion that we would respond to a situation with calmness and rationality. Conversely, we need to envisage a situation wherein we respond initially with apprehension and instinct, yet promptly regain composure, pose insightful inquiries that steer us towards contemplating alternative viewpoints and approaching the situation logically, and ultimately arrive at a judicious, informed choice.

In light of the aforementioned information, it is evident that NLP holds significant prowess in strategizing for future achievements, and we have observed several alternative methodologies for incorporating NLP techniques into our daily lives. Subsequently, we will examine various distinctive concepts in which we can employ NLP to enhance our well-being and eliminate negative influences.

## The Mechanisms, Locations, And Rationale Behind The Efficacy Of Neuro Linguistic Programming

Since its inception, NLP has maintained a primary emphasis on psychotherapy. Psychotherapy, known also as "verbal counseling," is a therapeutic approach aimed at assisting individuals with mental disorders in gaining insight into their condition. Psychotherapy equips individuals with the necessary resources to effectively manage stress, maladaptive cognition, and perilous conduct. Psychotherapists who specialize in the application of Neuro-Linguistic Programming (NLP ) frequently employ transformative methodologies to modulate behavior by altering ingrained patterns of thinking and behavior, with the aim of cultivating a more constructive cognitive orientation. An illustrative instance would involve identifying the favorable elements of a thought or behavior as opposed to fixating on the adverse aspects. Through this approach, patients can enhance their symptom management and optimize their functioning in their day-to-day activities. The concept can be likened to the phrase "input determines output." The content you choose to engage with, including negative individuals, aggressive discourse, or unsuitable conduct, will inevitably shape your thoughts and expressions.

It appears pertinent to note that while there are several, the primary therapeutic applications of NLP can be classified into two categories: Firstly, it is employed by therapists who specialize in various therapeutic domains including but not limited to disease management, preventative measures, obesity, autism, and rehabilitation. Secondly, NLP functions as an established therapeutic modality known as Neurolinguistic Psychotherapy, which has received recognition from the United Kingdom Council for Psychotherapy. Its accreditation is regulated by the Association for Neuro Linguistic Programming, and more recently, by its subsidiary body, the Neuro Linguistic Psychotherapy and Counseling Association. 8

A myriad of individuals and vocations, ranging from business professionals and healthcare practitioners to therapists, actors, athletes, politicians, law enforcement officials, parents, lawyers, and even in one's personal life, have extensively employed and applied the principles and techniques of NLP . Due to its insightful examination of the human subconscious, intellectual processes, aspirations, and apprehensions, NLP can be likened to a cognitive guidebook, enabling individuals to effectively attain their intended objectives. Therefore, when engaging in the study and application of NLP, individuals can effectively implement targeted competencies essential for making constructive decisions, fostering enhanced self-assurance in interpersonal interactions, eradicating detrimental behavioral cycles, dispelling pessimistic cognitions and influences, and attaining a more lucid comprehension of personal desires and the means to achieve them.

Natural Language Processing (NLP) has been employed to effectively alter the perspectives of patients regarding matters pertaining to their postoperative or post-accident rehabilitation. By fostering their focus on recuperation, maintaining a state of optimal health, reestablishing normalcy, and reintegrating all facets of their existence, NLP has demonstrated its efficacy in exerting transformative influence on patient mindset. It has been employed for the treatment of various medical conditions, including migraines, arthritis, Parkinson's disease, and even cancer. NLP proponents assert that it has the capacity to effectively alleviate a multitude of phobias, while also facilitating individuals in adopting healthier dietary practices, quitting smoking, engaging in regular exercise, and cultivating a positive relationship with food.

While Natural Language Processing is notably in high demand within the domains of career development and self-improvement, there exists a subset of trainers and practitioners who possess limited expertise in employing this technology for the purpose of medical condition healing. Inquiries should be directed towards individuals proficient in the field of NLP , with a particular emphasis on this matter. Undeniably, for cases of severe illness, it is imperative to seek guidance from a medical practitioner as well.

In diverse domains, such as the realm of sports, the empirical evidence consistently demonstrates that NLP can effectively inspire and enhance athletes' overall performance. Its proficient application assists athletes in surmounting critique and serves as a valuable support system in competition, where they are constantly impelled to outperform their fellow teammates.

NLP holds significant importance in the realm of business encompassing sales training, motivational speaking, and management training, among various other professions not explicitly mentioned. Specifically, its relevance is heightened when it comes to effective communication with the public or business counterparts. NLP has the capability to instill confidence in individuals who engage in public speaking, facilitating the cultivation of motivation for motivational speakers themselves, while simultaneously inspiring and uplifting the audience. Natural Language Processing has the potential to assist individuals in various professions in achieving their objectives and in positively altering undesired conduct within the professional setting. It has the potential to enhance the ability of salespeople to exert influence, persuade clients, and ultimately drive sales growth. Most significantly, it can assist in consolidating your principles so as to attain triumph in your profession, well-being, interpersonal connections, and familial dynamics, while also refining your perspectives on financial matters. Implementing natural language processing (NLP) techniques can enable companies to effectively select the most qualified candidates from a pool of applicants, establish robust alliances both internally and externally, foster intercultural communication, and cultivate a team of outstanding customer service representatives, thereby enhancing the overall quality of services provided by the organization. With the assistance of NLP , managers can effectively facilitate sales presentations, establish cohesive teams, amicably resolve conflicts, engage in team-building exercises, and enhance productivity.

In the realm of parenting, the application of NLP techniques proves instrumental in mitigating instances of tension both between parents and children, as well as between spouses. By adeptly discerning unproductive behaviors and delving into the deeper motivations behind them, NLP fosters the swift implementation of alternative responses, thereby fostering the establishment of strong interpersonal connections. NLP has the potential to allure compatible individuals to one's life, enhance marital dynamics, facilitate the envisioning and realization of one's desired self-image, and foster improved interpersonal communication within one's family and beyond.

NLP is imparted in educational programs focused on human resource development and business studies. Political representatives have employed its principles to alleviate tension, enhance communication with their constituents, and demonstrate effective leadership. NLP has been effectively employed within law enforcement agencies, as well as amongst both secular and religious therapists, artists, and entertainers. Indeed, individuals from various professions and diverse backgrounds have successfully applied the techniques and methodologies of NLP , yielding remarkable outcomes. Through the application of Natural Language Processing (NLP ), one can intellectualize their capabilities to a degree that exceeds their previous imaginings. The strategies and techniques provide a robust framework with boundless potential, constrained only by the limits of your own imagination.

Tony Robbins is widely recognized as a preeminent self-help coach and esteemed motivational speaker. Whether or not you are familiar with Tony Robbins, his name is widely recognized and he holds a prominent position in the field of NLP . Undoubtedly, his extensive contributions can be credited for the widespread popularity that NLP enjoys today. Implementing a select few (or ideally, all) of Tony's concepts and methodologies has the potential to yield significant outcomes in your daily existence.


Framing Positive Emotions

The prior counsel regarding the recontextualization of past adversities ought to have aided you in adopting a more dispassionate and impartial perspective towards past traumatic occurrences, thereby diminishing their emotional burden and enabling you to progress in your life. However, there are occasions when it becomes desirable to execute the antithesis, namely, presenting occurrences in a more optimistic light. This denotes that you will once more engage with past occurrences and circumstances, while enhancing their significance and impact on your being.

There are various motives for engaging in this act, such as the desire to augment a cherished recollection involving loved ones and companions. However, I found this strategy to be particularly beneficial in terms of my personal growth. I employed it to amplify instances of fleeting triumph into significantly more intricate illumination. Be mindful that these circumstances do not possess inherent significance by nature, but rather acquire the meanings that you choose to assign them.

From my perspective, the focus was centered on solidifying and eliciting additional favorable emotions associated with significant achievements in my professional endeavors. This approach served to propel further advancement and contribute to the reinforcement of positive patterns, ultimately amplifying my future success. One notable aspect of your life is the ability to employ NLP techniques, such as the ones mentioned, to meticulously shape and guide it towards any desired trajectory. Acquiring a handful of competencies and methodologies like these is all that is necessary to accomplish this task.

Returning to the topic of the positive framing strategy. When preparing for a significant or forthcoming occasion, such as an interview or business meeting, it is advisable to initially envisage oneself in an unadorned and vacant chamber. Subsequently, introspect on the question: 'How do I desire individuals to perceive me during the forthcoming occasion?' Contemplate the manner in which you wish to be regarded and acknowledged by others, as an individual.

The mental picture you possess shall serve as the foundation upon which you are commencing the creation of this image. Rather than exerting pressure, simply embark upon the construction of the scenario, concentrating on your movements, body language, and overall perception of your behavior. All aspects encompassing your orientation and attire.

Now observe as the visual narrative unfolds, portraying the highly favorable progression of events, wherein you adeptly preside over the meeting with poise and assurance. Individuals are demonstrating a deep level of satisfaction and admiration towards your method of articulation, and are potentially expressing their appreciation through gentle applause and accolades. Observe as you graciously receive the acclaim with a poised countenance and an upright posture.

Now, it is a matter of integrating this potent, assured, and composed depiction into the context and environment surrounding the forthcoming event/gathering. Immerse yourself in that particular setting, envision the imagery, including the vibrant hues and intricate textures of the space. In order to enhance your confidence, it is recommended to inhale the pleasant scent of your preferred fragrance on your person. Strive for utmost clarity and persuasiveness, envision yourself compelling each individual in the room with the power of your words. Observe their expressions as they engage in joyful laughter and exhibit joy in response to your humorous anecdotes or any other achievement you aspire to attain.

Now, enlarge this image to a diameter of 100 feet and observe it on an LCD screen positioned directly in front of you within the vacant chamber. It possesses a considerable size, occupying an entire wall. The subsequent course of action entails immersing oneself into the picture, seamlessly integrating with the digital image displayed on the screen. Gain firsthand perception of the circumstances, assuming the perspective of an observer who is fully engaged with all visual, auditory, and emotional stimuli, as if the events were unfolding in your immediate surroundings. Feel free to immerse yourself for as much time as you desire in the emotions evoked by the exceptionally self-assured and composed individual. This represents your authentic portrayal of yourself.

Feel free to practice this as frequently as you desire, and across a range of scenarios. It is advisable to develop the habit of empathizing with the perspective of individuals who are considered confident, as this behavior will become second nature to you given the frequency with which you have found yourself in similar situations. Once more, the human mind is unable to distinguish between a cognitively constructed scenario and an actual occurrence. You are effectively enriching your future film portfolio by incorporating emotionally impactful narratives of positivity and achievement. Upon arrival, one will find a sense of familiarity and naturalness, prompting the adoption of such behavior.

On occasion, I find it preferable to engage in retrospection with regards to adverse occurrences as well. I find that it enhances the aforementioned process of picture framing. Not only do I reinterpret the situation I perceived as unfavorable through an outdated and inconsequential lens, but I also derive pleasure from replaying select scenarios on a large display and envisioning them unfolding exceptionally. With sufficient repetition, the mind gradually establishes these novel neural connections and begins to diminish or, at the very least, minimize the negative aspects, while emphasizing them in a positive context.

This does not constitute self-deception in the sense of falsely claiming that you made that agreement when you did not, or asserting that you passed the exam when you actually failed. According to the procedural methodology, what you are doing is merely altering the perspective of the event from an emotional standpoint. You are effectively establishing a fresh perspective, one that is more advantageous for your interests.

This is feasible for any preceding or forthcoming circumstance of your preference. This approach is applicable to all perceived attributes of strength or weakness, making it possible to enhance the positive aspects and diminish the negative ones. The crucial factor lies in the process of deducing significance, over which you possess complete authority. Nothing possesses inherent significance; rather, it attains meaning solely through the subjective interpretation one assigns to it.

Engaging attentively and demonstrating authentic curiosity

Exerting influence on others during conversations is not contingent upon our external appearance, charm-based tactics, or verbal proficiency. In fact, the capacity to attentively listen to others is at the core of effectively exerting influence through communication. To clarify, it is imperative that we actively attend to the words conveyed by our counterpart during our discourse, rather than being preoccupied with our own utterances. NLP postulates that donning a $300 suit does not inherently result in the automatic capacity to adeptly exert influence or effectively engage in communication with others. On the contrary, NLP posits that your capacity to exert influence over others derives from the manner in which you cultivate a sense of safety and comfort in the individual during your discourse. Is their interest piqued by the content of your discourse? Have you demonstrated to them your genuine interest in their perspectives, emotions, and thoughts?

Applying NLP techniques:

On occasion, during interpersonal exchanges, individuals have a proclivity to engage in self-centered discussion. This tendency commonly manifests when one finds themselves in the presence of unfamiliar company or experiences discomfort within social settings, as they find solace in familiarizing themselves with their own life experiences. We are capable of discussing our own experiences and expressing ourselves with a sense of assurance. Nonetheless, when applying NLP techniques, it is imperative for us to refrain from succumbing to this inclination. To exert an impact on others during discourse, NLP posits that we should center the conversation primarily on the interlocutor, without imparting an interrogative undertone. Actively engaging in active listening, offering appropriate responses, and demonstrating authentic interest in another person's conversation facilitates a sense of comfort for them, likely prompting them to share additional information about the subject matter and become more open to our perspectives and suggestions. In the upcoming dialogue intended to exert influence or propose an idea, kindly take into consideration the subsequent recommendations and Neuro-Linguistic Programming (NLP) methodologies:

Sustain consistent eye contact and employ regular nodding as an act of conversational courtesy, as a mere nod has the power to effectively stimulate the continuation of an individual's discourse. The NLP technique is frequently employed by interviewers with the dual purpose of fostering a sense of ease in the interviewee and eliciting further elaboration or clarification in their responses. The greater one's knowledge, the more feasible it becomes to exert influence over others.

Inquire—whether you are seeking clarification regarding an individual or their statements, this act diminishes your own prominence and directs attention towards them. When an individual perceives a sincere interest on your part, they will impart additional information and demonstrate increased openness towards your ideas and opinions as you subtly introduce them. Ensure that your inquiries do not give the impression of conducting an interrogation.

Assume a stance where your feet are directed towards them—research has indicated that the positioning of our feet can frequently indicate our attentiveness or affinity towards someone. Typically an unconscious behavior, deliberately aligning your feet towards the individual you are engaged in conversation with will create the impression of utmost interest in their words. Engaging in a conversation while facing away from someone fails to fully demonstrate attentiveness. They will take note of this and display reduced willingness to disclose further personal or significant details to you, in addition to being unresponsive to your suggestions or ability to influence.

## Types Of Narcissism

Conversational Narcissism refers to a specific manifestation of narcissism observed in individuals who, due to their insatiable desire for attention, frequently divert the conversation away from its central topic towards themselves. They exhibit a noticeable lack of attention or complete disregard for the other party, instead focusing the conversation primarily on themselves. It is evident in casual exchanges and workplace dialogues. Over the years, there has been a rise in the discourse surrounding the propriety of attentive listening and engaging in meaningful dialogue. This trend indicates a prevailing prevalence of conversational narcissism in our daily interactions. However, this form of self-absorption typically manifests itself in subtle rather than overt ways, as many individuals now make a conscious effort to avoid being perceived as egotistical in conversations. Presented below is an illustration of a dialogue that reflects conversational narcissism in contrast to a dialogue that lacks narcissistic tendencies.

April: I am feeling quite melancholic today.

James: It is remarkable, April, how vibrant the sky appears today. Isn't today a splendid day? (Egocentric and fluctuating reaction)

April: I am feeling rather melancholic today.

James: O my dear. So sorry about that. What's the matter? (An empathetic and encouraging response).

In the initial hypothetical scenario, James endeavors to redirect the conversation away from April's emotions, despite the fact that she was the one who initiated the dialogue. This indicates that on a subconscious level,

James dismisses April's sadness as insignificant compared to his perception that it is a beautiful day due to the blue sky. It is characterized by the preoccupation with self that is so distinctive among individuals with narcissistic tendencies. In the latter response, James quickly grasps the situation, prompting him to demonstrate sufficient empathy to inquire about the cause of Jane's distress.

Cultural narcissism manifests itself on a wider societal level as a form of narcissism that is prevalent. This form of narcissism is distinguished by an exaggerated desire to amass wealth to the extent that it forsakes the common good in favor of self-serving personal benefits. This phenomenon is widely observed in numerous countries, where pervasive corruption and embezzlement prevail, as individuals prioritize personal enrichment over utilizing funds for infrastructure development and communal welfare. This phenomenon frequently has a detrimental impact on the populace and instills a profound feeling of deprivation. This phenomenon subsequently gives rise to various detrimental consequences, including the gradual erosion of the arts' capacity for liberation, as it is frequently tainted by instances of governmental corruption, wherein individuals are induced through bribery to employ it for their own agenda. In such societies, the media is inundated with unconstructive propaganda and manipulated to create the illusion that the government prioritizes the well-being of the populace, while consistently causing harm to them. The far-reaching consequences of a given situation lead to a considerable number of citizens even endorsing their oppressors. Should a person attempt to liberate them, a considerable segment of the population will instinctively resist their efforts.

## Destructive Narcissism

Malignant narcissism refers to a type of narcissism characterized by an individual's increasing self-centeredness and egotism as they achieve their desired goals and aspirations over time. The transformation of this type of narcissism can be likened to the proliferation of metastatic cancer cells through rapid and aggressive cellular division. As the malevolent Narcissist achieves greater success, his perception of his own value expands and his engagement in the pursuit of self-indulgence and conceit intensifies. He frequently displays a predisposition towards sociability and tends to gradually develop paranoid tendencies. This particular manifestation of narcissism is commonly referred to as such due to its attribution of a broader spectrum of symptoms, as compared to other variations of narcissism. These symptoms encompass paranoia, psychopathy, aggression, and sadism.

## Situations Where Narcissism Is Frequently Encountered

In the realm of professional relationships, we frequently encounter individuals displaying narcissistic tendencies within our workplace. They are individuals who consistently engage in counterproductive work behavior (CWB), which poses significant harm to the organization as a whole. And frequently, their motivations behind these actions stem from their desire for things to be executed according to their preferences, disregarding the more informed opinions of the general populace. They frequently exhibit sporadic reactions whenever it appears that their self-esteem is jeopardized.

Employers can display narcissistic tendencies, just like employees. Employees with a high degree of narcissism tend to perceive the conducts of their colleagues in the workplace as abusive and menacing, as opposed to individuals who have lower levels of narcissistic traits.

Proto-narcissism: This form of narcissism manifests during the initial developmental phase of an individual's life. The aforementioned pre-ego, which also corresponds to the id according to psychologists and psychiatrists, pertains to a form of narcissism. Typically, this occurs prior to the infant attaining any awareness or perception of others and its environment. Absence of this awareness renders it implausible to bestow affection upon others, as the person remains insufficiently attuned to the needs of others that elicit the blossoming of love. This form of narcissism pertains to the innate condition of an infant during the prenatal period and initial days of existence, prior to acquiring an understanding that other individuals exist beyond itself. Consequently, the infant remains oblivious to the presence of other sentient beings endowed with emotions. The chronology of this phenomenon diverges significantly from that of genuine narcissism.

Sexual Narcissism: Individuals afflicted with this type of narcissism typically possess an inflated perception of their sexual abilities. Frequently, individuals hold the belief that they possess a superior ability to provide sexual gratification to their partners, which often fails to align with the actuality of their performance. They also engage in promiscuous behavior as a means to seek fulfillment in order to compensate for their diminished self-worth and inability to establish genuine intimacy. Those individuals who are impacted by this form of narcissism frequently bear responsibility for instances of domestic violence. This form of Narcissism also gives rise to sexual addiction. Such a manifestation of narcissism exhibits a higher prevalence among males compared to females. Individuals who exhibit sexual narcissism frequently demonstrate excessive pride and an obsession with their own masculinity or femininity.

Conditions Under Which Narcissism Exists
The Phenomenon of Narcissism within the Realm of Parenting
Narcissism is also present in the realm of parenthood. Narcissistic parents are characterized by their strong desire to ensure their children conform to a specific set of behaviors, as they

perceive their children as extensions of themselves. They demonstrate a lack of genuine empathy towards their children, as a result, they frequently employ coercive tactics in order to compel their children to conform to their desires.

## Attract More Wealth

Each mental occurrence emits a cerebral frequency. The principle of the law of attraction is rooted in the underlying belief that a perpetual exchange exists between individuals and the cosmos. It can be deduced that the universe possesses consciousness. The meaning conveyed within the wavelength encapsulates our underlying purpose. Given that there is an interaction occurring between the universe and ourselves, it is highly probable that the universe will reciprocate our intentions and provide a corresponding response. If one consistently aspires to a promotion and diligently focuses on this intention through regular practice of meditation, it is probable that the cosmos will align to fulfill one's desires. Conversely, harboring adverse or pessimistic notions will yield unfavorable outcomes. Ultimately, harboring a negative mindset gives rise to apprehension. When we harbor uncertainty, the likelihood of events unfolding diminishes.

Napoleon Hill, the esteemed author who achieved great success and is widely acknowledged, postulated that, "The human mind has the capacity to manifest and accomplish anything it can imagine and have faith in." To effectively utilize the Law of Attraction, it is imperative that we not only entertain thoughts of fruition, but, above all, possess unwavering belief in the desired outcome.

Presented below are several measures that you can promptly undertake to achieve this objective:

1. Set up goals

In the practice of utilizing the Law of Attraction during meditation, it is essential that our intentions are supported by a distinct and precise objective. Precisely delineated outcomes facilitate the attainment of objectives without experiencing a sense of being inundated. The desire to amass wealth will not prove to be fruitful. If your intention is to achieve wealth, it is essential to develop a well-defined strategy or set of actions that will effectively pave the way towards that objective. One illustration could be: "By the month of December." On December 31st, 2014, I intend to establish a business venture that will yield significant financial gains. In order to accomplish this, I shall commit a duration of three hours per weekday (from 4pm to 7pm) towards its pursuit. This serves as a preliminary action plan, acknowledging the necessity for further refinement and precision. Consider this question: What specific tasks will I undertake during those designated hours? Then, proceed to establish precise deadlines that will enable you to make progress towards accomplishing your overarching objective.

Please procure a sheet of paper and transcribe all your aspirations and desires. Please refine your selection to prioritize the items that hold the greatest significance for you.

Your objectives serve as the fundamental core of the Law of Attraction. Avoid making sweeping generalizations and instead focus on being precise and formulating a detailed plan to achieve your desired outcome.

## 2. Altering your system of beliefs through the process of reframing

The foremost obstacle to achieving success lies within us. On the reverse side of the document, kindly enumerate any constraining convictions that could potentially impede the attainment of those objectives (e.g. "I am unworthy of success," "I lack sufficient intelligence," "I will never achieve weight loss," "I exhibit an inability to sustain focus for more than a minute," or "I perpetually fail in all endeavors," etc.). Engage in self-reflection, for it is solely through sincere purpose that we can transform aspirations into actuality.

These are our subjective beliefs concerning existence...that possess the potential to be modified or altered. Your objectives will not materialize if they are in conflict with your personal convictions. Despite our strong desire to attain success, the presence of even a single shadow of uncertainty regarding our capability to accomplish it has the potential to impede our progress towards achieving our objective.

Please peruse the reverse side of the document you have just written. The challenges that have been documented are ingrained beliefs. By employing the method known as framing, it is possible for us to modify those unfavorable thoughts and substitute them with more optimistic ones. The negative cannot be processed by the unconscious mind. Initially, it endeavors to construe the idea as impartial or favorable, subsequently seeking to invert it by utilizing the modifier "not" or incorporating a negative expression.

One might provide an instance of transforming a pessimistic statement into an optimistic one as follows: rather than stating, "Do not feel afraid," it would be more apt to express, "Exhibit courage." One can discern a notable discrepancy and influence between these two statements. Should you find yourself questioning your convictions, consider reflecting upon a point in your life when you demonstrated courage. For it is within the realm of human experience that each individual encounters instances where bravery becomes a necessary response or a deliberate choice. Consider the instances when you initially raised your hand to respond to a question during a classroom discussion, introduced yourself to an unfamiliar individual, or ventured to invite someone out for a romantic outing. In any case, the essence of the matter lies in expressing your desires, thereby enhancing their visibility and augmenting the probability of their realization.

In order to frame, it is necessary to begin by closing one's eyes and mentally envisioning oneself. Envision yourself as a character in a motion picture. You hold the position of director and possess the authority to determine the course of action within it. Consider reflecting upon your constraints or pessimistic convictions and subsequently reversing them. As an illustration, the statement "I am unable to lose weight" can be reframed as "I have the ability to achieve weight loss." Similarly, the declaration "I am incapable of doing anything correctly" may be transformed into "I possess the capability to accomplish tasks proficiently." Subsequently, it is imperative to internalize and put into practice this conviction within the context of one's own narrative or personal development. In reality, envision yourself undertaking the task and challenging your own self-imposed limitations. You may freely extend the duration of the movie as desired. You have just exemplified your capacity for improvement. Observe keenly and affirm to yourself that you possess the ability to reproduce the images witnessed in the imaginative visual experience.

Engaging in a cognitive exercise where you envision the desired response in your thoughts will greatly enhance the likelihood of its occurrence. The utilization of framing proves advantageous in constructing a distinct and alternate reality, subsequently implementing it within the realm of an individual's personal experiences.

## 3. Meditate

Once an individual has positioned themselves as proficient in their aspirations, they truly possess the conviction that they are capable of attaining them, whether by transcending self-imposed limitations or accomplishing objectives.

Each morning, make a deliberate effort to retreat to a tranquil space, assume a seated position, and allocate a brief duration of five to ten minutes for contemplation regarding your particular objective, as well as strategizing methods to advance towards its attainment throughout the course of the day. One may choose to employ soft music as a means of fostering an appropriate emotional ambiance, or alternatively, utilize a mantra to induce a state of tranquility and mental calmness.

Envision the presence of currency in your surroundings. Strive to cultivate a proactive and optimistic mindset to enhance productivity.

When employing the Law of Attraction, we experience heightened assurance that the objectives we aspire to attain align authentically with our true desires. The realization of your goals will not materialize overnight; it necessitates the virtues of perseverance, resolve, and unwavering commitment in order to actualize them.

The Responsibilities of a Therapist" "The Duties of a Therapist" "The Functions of a Therapist" "The Obligations of a Therapist" "The Tasks of a Therapist
Therapists are individuals who provide assistance to their clients in addressing psychological concerns. Initially, they

provide guidance to foster the development of the community. This can be achieved through the provision of guidance and support to the community regarding sensitive topics, such as the experience of depression following the loss of a prominent community member. They assist the community in navigating challenging and extraordinary circumstances. They contribute to the enhancement of community bonding and motivate community members to stay vigilant and alert. Furthermore, this also serves to foster a resilient and robust community in all aspects. Additionally, they instill a sense of hope within the community they reside and operate in.

Therapists assume the role of a mediator between the client and their issues. It is the responsibility of the therapist to provide appropriate guidance in order to address the current issue effectively.

For instance, in the context of individuals seeking recovery from substance abuse, carefully structured guidelines are provided to enable them to abstain from alcohol or illicit substances. The therapist is expected to guide the client through the entire therapy session until its conclusion. The duration of the therapy may be extended as achieving change does not occur promptly. The therapist assumes a role akin to an individual who provides unwavering support to the client throughout the entire process.

A therapist is expected to serve as a steadfast source of emotional support for the client. It is imperative for the therapist to possess a genuine capacity for empathy. The individual in question must endeavor to empathize with the perspective of the client. This is intended to facilitate ongoing client engagement. This demonstrates a profound sense of care and comprehension towards the situation. The therapist must refrain from engaging in any form of mockery towards the client. The purpose of this is to prevent the client from discontinuing therapy and forgoing treatment at the therapist's practice. It is imperative that he exhibits gentleness and benevolence, and in the event that he does not possess these qualities, it is incumbent upon him to acquire a disposition characterized by compassion.

It is imperative for the therapist to serve as a catalyst for implementing the recommendations they make to their clients. In instances where an individual with substance abuse issues is assigned a task, it becomes the responsibility of the therapist to assess its completion. It is imperative that the therapist oversees the advancement of the client. The therapist may also assess the clients' progress by inquiring with their family members and close acquaintances. The work of a therapist is never truly completed, as even after the therapy sessions have concluded, it is their responsibility to follow up and monitor the progress of their clients.

The therapists should facilitate a secure environment for the client's recovery, taking into consideration their family background and social network, if applicable. The responsibility of the therapist lies in ensuring the safety, comfort, and compassion for their clients. Additionally, he can seek assistance to support him throughout the entirety of his therapy, as well as afterward. The therapist must respectfully intervene in the affairs of their clients while maintaining strict adherence to non-disclosure guidelines. Life under the guidance of a therapist is thoroughly attended to. The therapist assumes the role of a confidant and support system for the client, navigating the challenges of their life journey, which can be distressing.

## How Helpful is Therapy?

Therapy serves to address inquiries that arise within an individual's life, often achieved by delving into their subconscious realm to unveil and explore the unresolved aspects of their personal history. An additional benefit is that individuals gain a deeper self-awareness through discussing their own experiences. This helps to enhance mental and physical well-being in all facets of life. The therapists pose a query that challenges the client's perspective and prompts them to reflect on their daily decisions, thereby motivating them to strive for self-improvement in the interest of the collective welfare. This enables us to gain a fresh and comprehensive insight into the client.

In addition, therapy enables individuals to establish a deep connection with an external individual with whom they can openly confide without any apprehension. The therapist has committed to maintaining silence and can only communicate through written notes with the client's consent. This enables clients to establish a rapport with therapists without apprehension, thereby fostering a sense of closeness between individuals and their therapists. The client finds it effortless to establish a strong bond with his or her therapist due to their affectionate and sensitive demeanor. This is beneficial for the client's therapy journey, as well as for their post-therapy experience.

Therapy serves as a catalyst for bringing diverse individuals together. This could potentially be located within the therapist's workplace. The client may encounter other clients who are receiving treatment from the same therapist, or may have interactions with other therapists who are professional colleagues of their assigned therapist. Engaging with unfamiliar individuals leads to the development of fresh connections. This could potentially signify the beginning of a fresh bond, whether it be a new friendship or a new close relationship. This recurring phenomenon of life is readily evident as a direct outcome of an individual's therapeutic interventions. This sustains and maintains an individual's existence. Each individual client acquires their own set of benefits as therapy progresses.

## Effective Natural Language Processing Techniques With The Potential To Transform Your Life

NLP 's scope has significantly expanded and evolved from its early years of application. This signifies that methodologies which may have been effective during the Bandler and Grinder era in the 1970s and 1980s may not be as applicable in contemporary times. To assist you in discerning valuable insights, enclosed are a collection of empirically validated NLP methodologies that you can effectively utilize to initiate transformative outcomes within your personal sphere as well as the broader spheres of influence.

*Dissociation

It is not unprecedented for individuals to respond excessively to a situation or action, subsequently fixating on and lamenting their impulsive actions. This is where the phenomenon of dissociation exerts significant influence. It facilitates the elimination of detrimental emotions and cognitive patterns, thereby enabling a more objective perception of the situation. Professionals within the phobia domain also employ this methodology in order to effectively treat phobias. "To engage in a dissociation technique:

Firstly, commence the process by discerning the specific emotion or stimulus that is inducing distress and impacting your emotional state in an adverse manner.

Second step- Envision yourself as an impartial observer adeptly overcoming the situation (the key is to contemplate how an individual unaffected by any phobia would effectively manage the situation).

Third Step- This stage entails the ongoing repetition of step two, with the inclusion of a few additional favorable attributes to enhance the virtual representation of oneself. Additionally, it is permissible for you to incorporate humor into the virtual context or incorporate musical elements.

Proceed to step four: Gain a visual perception of the situation from a current standpoint. The actions performed in steps 1-3 ought to have altered the stimulus or rendered it nonexistent. If you do not experience any inclination towards this, please proceed to repeat the procedure.

*Content Reframe

There may be certain circumstances in life that induce a profound sense of powerlessness and elicit a detrimental emotional response. If such a scenario exists, employing the NLP technique of content reframing could be advantageous. It transforms the connotation of an unfavorable circumstance into a favorable one. For instance, an individual, hereby referred to as Joe, was deprived of his employment today. Naturally, he would be overwhelmed by devastation and perceive his existence as coming to an abrupt end. Nevertheless, should he choose to implement a content reframe approach to his circumstances, he would likely perceive the situation as a favorable chance to secure improved employment or initiate an independent entrepreneurial endeavor. Content reframing facilitates a shift in perspective, enabling one to adopt a more optimistic outlook by focusing on the positive aspects of situations. The key to executing this methodology lies in substituting all forms of negativity with elements of positivity. To illustrate, in the case of aviophobia, instead of contemplating the prospect of an aircraft encountering a calamitous accident in the sea, one may choose to envision an exceedingly vigilant and concerned flight attendant.

*Self Anchoring
In the field of NLP , the technique of self-anchoring is employed to trigger a desired emotional reaction in response to a specific action or verbal expression. An illustrative instance can be observed in the capacity to evoke a pleasant response, such as a smile, from an individual held dear, merely through the act of tenderly placing a hand on their arm or embracing them. The methodology is highly efficacious as it permits individuals to modify their emotional state in real-time. For instance, employing this method can enable one to transform sensations of panic into a sense of confidence when

embarking on their flight. Furthermore, the approach is effective in addressing detrimental emotions by introducing a positive anchor, thereby altering one's emotional state within the given context. Allow me to provide you with a concise outline delineating the sequential measures involved in the process of anchoring.

Firstly, ascertain the desired emotional state that you wish to cultivate, such as courage, happiness, and the like. This component assumes a crucial function as it is unattainable to comprehend one's emotional state devoid of any inclination towards its nature. Determining your intended emotional state simplifies the process of establishing a viable path towards attaining it.

Secondly, undertake all necessary actions to elicit the desired emotional state. To illustrate, in the pursuit of happiness, one may deliberately wear a smile or actively endeavor to be in cheerful environments.

Proceeding to the third step, once you have achieved the emotional state you desire, employ the technique of visualizing a smoke circle and subsequently position yourself inside it. Envision the wisps of smoke emanating from the circle as a metaphor for the desired emotion enveloping your being. Revel in its exalted magnificence and dwell amidst the vaporous haze.

Progress to the fourth step- Effortlessly shift your focus away from the immediacy of the visual circle and intentionally redirect your thoughts towards any other subject unrelated to the emotions encapsulated within the smoke circle.

Proceed to the fifth step by reentering the smoke circle after a brief period of absence and observe your current emotional disposition. In the event that the exercise proved to be effective, you are likely to encounter the same emotions that were previously encountered.

*Rapport

Rapport refers to the ability to engage in conversations with individuals in diverse settings and contexts. Mastering this skill is a task of minimal complexity when one adheres to the appropriate procedural steps. Regrettably, there exist several methods of producing this. A highly efficacious method is to replicate the posture, or body language, of the individual with whom you are engaged in conversation. However, it is important to note that in certain social contexts, such an approach may not be deemed suitable. Hence, it is advisable to ensure that the mirror effect is discreet and imperceptible to scrutiny.

*Belief Change
An individual's efficacy in applying NLP frequently hinges upon their belief system, which often acts as a significant constraining factor. NLP is characterized by three primary constraints.
#Beliefs about cause
#Beliefs about meaning
#Beliefs about identity.
Beliefs encompass one's individual perspectives and encompass one's

approach towards experiences that deviate from one's belief structure. The convictions you hold are accountable for preserving your consciousness of the underlying verities inherent in the beliefs you adopt.

Convictions hold significant influence in shaping our existence, as they dictate the quality of life we encounter and embrace. Additionally, our convictions are shaped by the life experiences that we encounter. Consequently, if one fixates on adverse events from their past, there is a likelihood of perpetuating the attraction of unfavorable experiences. Nevertheless, through the application of the aforementioned content-reframe technique, the formation of negative beliefs and emotions will be rendered ineffective. This aligns with the principles espoused by the law of attraction, wherein concentrating on negativity leads to the attraction of negative outcomes. Additionally, it is imperative for me to acknowledge that there are discrepancies within our belief system in terms of evaluating circumstances. Indeed, there exist no situations that can be categorically deemed as either favorable or unfavorable. Our cognitive framework is such that we tend to categorize situations as unfavorable. This is precisely why one individual may perceive poverty as a misfortune, while another may consider it as a window of opportunity for personal advancement.

In order to alter negative beliefs, it is imperative to accumulate positive information pertaining to the circumstances rather than fixating on the negative aspects. Subsequently, it is imperative to thoroughly assess all relevant data, encompassing any adverse information. This facilitates the process of scrutinizing their credibility. In lieu of this, you may choose to eradicate negative beliefs through the practice of positive affirmation exercises. Positive affirmation entails engaging in a meditative practice within a serene environment, wherein one directs their unwavering attention towards the chosen affirmation. I have observed that mindfulness meditation techniques are effective in facilitating the formation of a mental representation aimed at reinforcing the newfound conviction. To cultivate a positive transformation in your life, it is imperative to concentrate on the affirmation phrase and its underlying significance, thereby executing the exercise. Mindfulness meditation yields remarkable results due to its ability to induce a state akin to hypnosis, enabling profound concentration on healing and the internalization of empowering affirmations at a subconscious level. This exercise is effective in enabling individuals to transcend any phobia, regardless of its magnitude, within a short duration of 10 to 15 days.

# Attain Success By Utilizing NLP Modeling

The foundations of NLP were established through the process of studying and emulating accomplished individuals in their respective domains. The methodologies employed in the modeling of these experts have transformed into the very instruments that facilitate the enhancement of intricate modeling procedures.

Success

What sets the founders Richard Bandler and John Grinder apart from typical researchers is their ability to discern the underlying structures and internal processes, often hidden from the models themselves, rather than focusing solely on technical skills as other researchers do. It is through this approach that they have unlocked the secret sauce, so to speak, that makes these individuals exemplary.

The inherent issue with these experts lies in their erroneous attribution of their success to their external skill sets rather than their internal game methodologies. The objective of modeling is to discern these imperceptible structures, examine them, and construct a model that can be imparted and replicated.

To achieve proficiency, let alone mastery, in a particular field, it is imperative to possess the necessary training and experiences. The limitation associated with modeling is the inability to instill the expertise of an accomplished fighter pilot solely by transferring the internal workings of a model. This is unless the individual possesses the fundamental capacity to perform reasonably well as a jet pilot, although not exceptionally so.

On the contrary, the structures that can be extracted from a well-established model are transferable to individuals operating outside the confines of the same field. Emulating the characteristics of an expert aviator can potentially translate effectively to a professional racing driver or even a law enforcement officer, depending on which specific traits were personified.

## The Three Stages of Modeling

### Observation

This entails a meticulous examination of the model and a heightened sensory perception to discern the internal mechanisms unfolding within the subject. This is where additional NLP tools are essential!

The integration of comprehensive natural language processing techniques to precisely analyze and deconstruct the different components, metacognitions, and processes, personal values, self-concepts, beliefs, capabilities, drivers, and so on. It represents an interactive procedure in which the acquisition of pertinent details through pinpoint information elicitation is required for the extraction of all conceivable valuable data.

### Critical Success Factors of the Model (The Distinctive Catalyst)

There exist only a limited number of elements that attribute to the exceptional performance of top performers. The difficulty lies in discerning which specific factors genuinely contribute to the brilliance of the model.

As an illustration, in the case where a medical professional (the exemplar) demonstrates remarkable proficiency, bearing in mind their dual expertise as a military medic and exceptional aptitude in mathematics, coupled with a degree in engineering.

Does the model's high level of mathematical intelligence or his battlefield experience as a combat medic account for his adeptness in addressing the medical problem effortlessly? Alternatively, could it be attributed to his "survive at all costs" mentality and the streamlined custom treatment protocols he utilized to save lives in the war zone? Alternatively, it could be neither. It is possible that the physician's heightened intuition affords him superior discernment compared to ordinary doctors, thereby enabling him to provide more efficient and effective treatment to patients, resulting in reduced mortality rates. The aforementioned data shall be gathered, subjected to analysis and refinement to eliminate irrelevant details, and subsequently examined to ascertain outcomes.

Approach to the Transfer of the Model

After obtaining the data, which includes the sequencing of the model's internal processes, it is essential that the developed model be transferable and capable of being taught.

One should not anticipate a precise replication of the model-subject's performance due to unaccounted variances, individuality, situational distinctiveness, and so forth; nevertheless, a significant proportion of the model-subject's distinctive processes and outcomes ought to be transferable and reproducible to ascertain the success of the model.

Nevertheless, the wrongdoer entrusts himself to the care of an unfamiliar hypnotherapist. It is highly improbable that you would jeopardize your life and well-being.

If an individual approaches you and claims to have the ability to induce a trance, it is advisable to refrain from allowing such an individual to attempt this on you unless you are in a suitable state. Primarily, it is essential to have trustworthy individuals managing you.

I originate from my accumulated knowledge.

One of the primary factors is the state of being secluded. This circumstance pertains to the state of being significantly distanced from one's family, acquaintances, and all that is familiar.

One cannot underestimate the gravity of the situation; however, experiencing social isolation can have a profound impact on one's psychological well-being. It is not only asserted that one is self-formed, but also shaped into the collective identity of a group that consists of individuals lacking autonomy.

Given the absence of someone to evict him, he would have preferred nothing more than to be with the famed child. To elucidate this matter, it would be wise to seek a resolution that distinguishes you from your familial and friendly acquaintances.

Please ensure your ability to collaborate with me.

It encompasses everything, ranging from menacing dangers to enigmatic mosquitoes. This intellect possesses the ability to manipulate circumstances over a prolonged period, leaving no room for uncertainty that it is the most perilous of them all.

Whenever you encounter a risk, it is essential that you solicit the assistance of your acquaintances, relatives, and the appropriate individual. Under normal circumstances, the plan is unlikely to lead to any form of success whatsoever.

These ideas possess the capability to manipulate and influence the human mind, a process that is deemed exceedingly challenging to counteract. Nevertheless, by means of conscious acknowledgment and assistance, one is able to refrain from perilous circumstances and establish certainty regarding the appropriate course of action.

## Increase Energy

It is quite remarkable to observe the correlation between our moods and our level of energy. Adverse and somber dispositions can amalgamate to cultivate a recurring mindset.
What is even more remarkable and potentially disconcerting is the manner in which our moods exert an influence on our levels of energy. The nature of our thoughts and the extent to which we ruminate on them will ultimately dictate whether we experience fatigue and weariness, or vitality and attentiveness.
Indeed, it is possible to experience fatigue following an extended period of work during the day. Frequently, fatigue is experienced due to a mistaken perception of tiredness.

Is it conceivable that this assertion could hold validity? Might one's emotional state and perspective significantly impact their daily energy levels? Can this be considered purely speculative?

According to the prevailing perspective in the field of NLP , personal experiences are regarded as more persuasive than empirical research. It is imperative to conduct comprehensive testing, encompassing all elements, including this particular item. This task can be accomplished within a brief span of minutes.

Analyze these situations in order to determine how your emotional state can impact your level of vigor. It is imperative that you engage in these activities rather than solely consuming information about them.

Peruse the narrative for each given scenario and subsequently devote a brief amount of time to contemplation. In order to eliminate it, one should consider standing up and engaging in physical activity.

Proceed with each individual scenario.

Scenario One

Kindly allocate a brief period to unwind and avail yourself of the opportunity to partake in this experience:

It currently marks the midpoint of the winter season, and the day in question happens to be Monday, specifically in the morning.

The weather is characterized by overcast conditions, diminished sunlight, precipitation, and low temperatures. You can perceive the sound of passing traffic. It is evident that you have a considerable workload awaiting you upon your arrival at work due to the absence of a fellow colleague who is currently on vacation, necessitating your duty to take over their responsibilities for the duration of this week.

Upon your arrival at work, it is necessary for you to participate in a tedious two-hour meeting. You proceed to inspect your correspondence and come across an invoice for your credit card. The amount is significantly greater than what you had anticipated."

Presently, what is your emotional state?

What level of energy do you currently perceive within yourself? "If you were in this situation, would you:

Prepare yourself to encounter and confront the challenges presented in your work?

View the world with a pleasant countenance.

Maintain a buoyant gait as you proceed on foot?

Engaging in frequent trips up and down the staircase?

Be bouncing around?

Probably not. Numerous individuals will experience a sense of exhaustion, demoralization, and melancholy when contemplating these matters.

Now, please rise and engage in physical activity. Prepare yourself for what is to come.

Scenario Two

This situation exhibits some divergence. It is identical to the preceding day in all aspects, barring a solitary distinction...

It is currently the midst of winter and the present time is Monday morning.

The weather is characterized by an overcast sky, lack of sunlight, precipitation, and low temperatures. You perceive the sound of passing traffic. It is apparent that a significant amount of work awaits you upon arriving at the workplace, as one of your colleagues is currently on vacation and you are tasked with assuming their responsibilities for the duration of this week.

Upon your arrival at the workplace, it is expected that you will also be required to participate in a tedious and lengthy meeting that spans two hours. Just prior to your departure for work, you receive some delightful news...

An individual whom you have held a longstanding affinity for has extended a message to you, expressing an inclination to convene at some point during the current week.

What impact will this have on your professional duties?

What is your current level of energy?

Do you experience a sensation of weightlessness or heaviness?

You have been granted a substantial sum of money. The size of the amount is not significant enough to warrant you quitting your job, although you will have ample possibilities for its utilization.

What sentiments are currently occupying your thoughts?

Will this have an impact on your productivity and energy levels at work?

Has this elicited a smile from you?

You have recently received a telephone call regarding the interview you attended last week, and as a result, your aspiration of securing your ideal job is now within grasp. You will commence this new phase in precisely four weeks' time.

Does this instill in you a desire to report for duty?

Are you enthusiastically leaping in jubilation?

What is the extent of your physical vitality?

Your significant other has just provided you with a telephone update after attending a medical consultation, conveying the news of her pregnancy.

You have made persistent efforts over an extensive period.
Could this have an impact on your overall professional efficiency?
How are you currently experiencing your emotions?
What is the current state of your mood?
To what extent does your disposition vary between receiving unfavorable and favorable news?
Wishing you a day filled with invigorating experiences.
Please do not simply wish for a pleasant day, but instead, may your day be filled with thought-provoking and engaging experiences. Our thought processes and the content of our thoughts have a significant impact on your overall energy levels. Consistently exhibiting a pessimistic and despondent attitude will gradually diminish your optimism if you fail to attend to the manner in which you approach each day.
Wait, there's more...
It can prove to be a challenging endeavor to maintain an optimistic and cheerful disposition solely through

mental effort. It does not solely revolve around cognitive faculties. It is imperative to effectively regulate the manner in which you lead your daily life, ensuring that your activities and routines contribute to both your physical and mental stimulation.

Fortunately, this does not imply that you must rise earlier and engage in an exhaustive workout regimen prior to commencing your workday.

Body Affects Mind

It is not uncommon for individuals to experience intermittent periods of overwhelming fatigue. On certain occasions, individuals may have a rationale, such as instances when one has been diligently exerting effort, undergoing significant mental strain, or engaging in rigorous physical exercise.

At times, the mere experience of navigating the routines and challenges of everyday life can lead to both physical and mental fatigue.

We tend to fall into patterns and become preoccupied with the aspects that are not going well in our lives or the potential negative outcomes. This has an impact on our locomotion, posture, and stance. We begin slumping over. We walk slower. Our faces aren't animated. The force of gravity creates a sensation akin to being pulled downward.

These physiological and psychological tendencies attain a state of normality. Our perspective will undergo a transformation, leading us to believe that "this is my current state" while attributing it solely to our genetic makeup or the passage of time. This pessimistic viewpoint will inevitably yield additional corroborative evidence.

What Can We Do?

A commonly held viewpoint asserts that the singular solution to address this issue is the modification of one's dietary habits. Indeed, on occasion, fatigue may stem from a deficiency in vitamin C and B, potassium, or magnesium. I have not encountered anyone who has successfully alleviated this form of fatigue through the use of dietary supplements. It would be advisable for you to adhere to a nutritious dietary regimen and maintain a consistent meal schedule.

Alternative phrasings in formal tone: 1. It is commonly advised by others that engaging in physical exercise is necessary. 2. The general consensus is that incorporating exercise into your routine is imperative, according to various individuals. 3. The prevailing viewpoint among others is that regular exercise is a prerequisite. 4. It has been widely propagated by others that maintaining a consistent exercise regimen is indispensable. 5. The prevailing sentiment upheld by others is that one should prioritize physical exercise. This proposal is commendable as well, although one must acknowledge that contemplating physical activity while already experiencing fatigue amplifies the sensation of weariness. The solution may entail uncomplicated and straightforward actions: gradually making efforts to break free from your monotonous routine.

Stop After Satisfied

Cease consumption once satiety is achieved.

Consume food when experiencing physical hunger and conclude eating once feeling satiated. Hungry has different stages. In order to facilitate the identification of incidences of hunger and starvation, we can employ a hunger scale. The spectrum ranges from a rating of one to ten, encompassing extreme hunger to complete satiety.

1. Starving
Dizzy and light-headed. You experience sensations of weakness or tremors, accompanied by an intense desire to consume sustenance, with thoughts entirely focused on the act of eating.

2. Extremely hungry.
You are experiencing intense hunger and are in need of nourishment. You begin to exhibit a touch of irritability and are probably preoccupied with thoughts of sustenance.

3. Hungry.
You experience feelings of hunger and eagerly anticipate the consumption of food. One's stomach is rumbling, and there could be a sensation of acidity.

4. Slightly hungry.
Experience slight pangs of hunger in advance. You are capable of partaking in sustenance, but you are aware that you can exercise patience and postpone it for a brief period.

5. Satisfied.
In a state of equilibrium, devoid of both hunger and satiety. In order to achieve weight loss, it is necessary to refrain from consuming food at this establishment.

6. Comfortable.
Your physique experiences a sense of satisfaction derived from the nourishment.

7. Slightly uncomfortable full.

The body has indicated its satiety, yet you persist in consuming food.

8. Feeling stuffed.
Consume an excessive amount of food and experience mild discomfort in your stomach.

9. Very uncomfortable.
It appears that you are consuming excessive amounts of food, and it may be advisable to consider adjusting your attire for increased comfort.

10. So overwhelmingly satiated that you experience a feeling of discomfort.
You have consumed an excessive amount of food and are experiencing physical discomfort, making it challenging to suppress the urge to vomit.

The hunger scale aids in determining the appropriate commencement and cessation of your meals. It is imperative to ensure that one consumes food solely for the purpose of alleviating hunger and restoring energy to the body. It is advisable to consume an amount of food that is sufficient to satiate your appetite. It would be preferable to commence the consumption of food when one's hunger level is around a magnitude of three or four, and discontinue eating when the sensation of hunger reaches a level of approximately five or six. Cease consumption once you have reached a satiety level of five, indicating that your caloric intake is adequate and preventing excessive overeating.

Cease consumption once a sense of satiation is experienced. During the process of eating, the stomach sends a sensory signal to indicate that the body has obtained an adequate amount of energy from the consumed foods. Based on the conducted research, it has been found that the duration required for the brain to relay a message to the stomach indicating satiety is approximately 20 minutes. If one consumes their food at an excessively rapid pace, it is likely that by the time the body sends the signal indicating satiety, an excessive amount of food will have already been ingested. However, when one adopts a deliberate and unhurried approach to eating, they can effectively regulate their food intake upon receiving a cue. It is advised to consume your meals at a leisurely pace and thoroughly chew your food.

It is recommended to masticate your food for a minimum of 30-40 times prior to ingestion. The majority of individuals are unaware that the process of digestion commences in the oral cavity. When food is thoroughly masticated, it facilitates the body's ability to effectively decompose and subsequently assimilate all essential nutrients. By thoroughly masticating your food, it allows for increased temporal awareness within your cerebral function, thereby facilitating the recognition of satiety. It will not solely contribute to weight loss, but also serve to improve your digestive processes.

Commence the process of developing trust in the signals that your body provides, and diligently observe and acknowledge the input from each of your five senses during the act of consuming food. While consuming your meal, direct your attention solely towards the food and relish its flavors. Please take a seat and partake in your meal. Kindly refrain from engaging in any distractions while eating. It is vital to avoid multitasking during your mealtime and abstain from watching, reading, or working while dining. Should you become preoccupied, you may encounter the inclination to overindulge in food. Direct your exclusive attention towards the culinary aspects, encompassing the taste, aroma, and tactile sensations of the food.

Engage in cultivating self-awareness of bodily sensations. During the act of dining, it is advisable to consistently inquire within oneself, "Have I consumed an adequate amount?" It is suggested to engage in this introspection approximately five minutes following the consumption of half of one's current serving. Pose the question to yourself regarding whether the subsequent mouthful will enhance or diminish your well-being. It might present challenges for individuals accustomed to disregarding their bodily cues. If you have adhered to a dietary regimen for a considerable duration, you have been accustomed to consuming meals in accordance with their prescribed guidelines. You have been accustomed to disregarding the physiological cues of your body, be it hunger or satiation. Consequently, you have disregarded the physiological cue from your body.

Should you indeed encounter difficulty in recognizing the signals of your own body, it is advisable to make an initial estimation. Acquiring the ability to attentively perceive one's bodily sensations may necessitate a period of a few days. There is no cause for concern regarding the accuracy of your guesses. In the event of an incorrect guess, take solace in the knowledge that it will enhance your future accuracy.

What would happen if, upon reaching the point of satiation, I have not consumed all of the remaining food? Inherently, the human body was designed to consume food when experiencing hunger and cease consumption once the feeling of satiety is reached. The majority of individuals cease consuming once they have exhausted all the food items on their plate. A widely held belief among individuals is that it is considered rude to squander food. A significant portion of us have been instructed to consume all the food served to us. Our parents frequently reminded us to complete our meal. Therefore, regardless of the quantity of food presented to us, we will consume each and every portion, even after our satiation has been achieved.

Once you have reached a state of contentment, even if you have not entirely consumed your meal, it is advisable to refrain from further indulgence. If you possess a aversion to wasting food, consider partaking in smaller portions. In the event that your sense of satisfaction remains unfulfilled, it may be suitable to consume an additional reduced amount. Alternatively, you may choose to store the remaining food in the refrigerator for future consumption. However, if you decide to dine at the restaurant and are unable to have your food taken away, your sole option would be to abandon your meal. This task presents inherent challenges due to the multifaceted nature of influence from parental teachings, alongside the potential emergence of feelings of guilt.

However, it is crucial to keep in mind your ultimate objective. Your objective is to maintain a state of good health and achieve weight reduction. If you hold a genuine appreciation for your physical well-being, it is recommended that you abstain from overindulging in food. If you experience profound remorse regarding the act of wasting food, may I suggest an appropriate course of action? Certainly, one may effectively address the sensation of guilt through the application of Emotional Freedom Techniques (EFT).

## Blackpool Rock

The essence of rock-candy resides in its inherent sweetness, while we, on the other hand, have the potential to embody bitterness. An essential aspect of making progress entails examining the inner thoughts and perceptions that you believe define your identity and behavior. If these aspects are considered unfavorable, one can discern the necessary steps to transform them into favorable attributes. Consequently, the transformation provides you with a detailed plan to adhere to during your individual reconstruction.

Blackpool rock is a confectionery originating from Britain, comprising primarily of sugar. This material undergoes a process of tugging and extending until it acquires sufficient elasticity to be rolled into shape. Various hues of letters are incorporated onto the extended block, and subsequently the entire entity is rolled and stretched to shape an elongated cylinder.

Blackpool rock holds a notable reputation, although it is not exclusive to the renowned seaside resort located in the Northwest of England.

Do we resemble the solidified mass that encompasses written expressions deeply ingrained within us, or can we alter the characters to compose alternative messages?

If you were bisected akin to a stick of rock, which words would be discerned by onlookers. When we reach a breaking point or experience a rupture, what are the verbal expressions that become divulged to the public sphere?

However, instead of being fragile and artificial, we possess a pliant nature and persevere in our growth and advancement.

Our encounters possess the ability to shape the inner workings of our being, while our actions hold the power to shape the external image projected unto others.

The contemplation of intrinsic evil poses a formidable challenge. Our individual dispositions may be influenced by the experiences we have encountered throughout our lives; nevertheless, it is important to acknowledge that we have the ability to articulate the expressions that are representative of our true selves. We have the opportunity to inspire and motivate others to assist us in crafting the constructive narrative in which we aspire to establish our reputation.

We are never fixed. I have a recollection of encountering a compassionate German couple, a married pair, who diligently placed floral tributes on the burial sites of Allied aviators. These aviators, in their attempt to conduct bombardment operations against Germany during the course of the Second World War, were unfortunately intercepted and downed.

The sentiments ingrained within their hearts and spirits are those of forgiveness. They comprehended that the actions of those youthful individuals were driven by an inherent commitment to their country. They were cognizant of the fact that the true antagonist was considerably distanced from the perils at hand.

BREATH

It is possible that we have long been aware of the correlation between respiration and tranquility, as well as inner harmony, yet regrettably overlooked the indicators.

The Earth was intricately crafted by the Great Architect, resulting in an unparalleled masterpiece.

All essential ingredients for its development and growth were incorporated, save for one crucial element. The creator delicately exhaled upon it while observing.

Upon the occasion that Breath found a dwelling, it exhaled a sigh of solace. It had actively sought out a suitable place of residence for an extended duration. Now, it beheld a location that appeared to be in dire need of some inspiration. It selected that lifeless and desolate celestial body aimlessly adrift amidst the cosmos. The inspiration converged and ultimately alighted upon it.

The comprehension of respiration presents an intriguing concept for our comprehension. It possesses the capability to endure within minuscule crevices, as well as to occupy vast expanses. It represents a boundless multitude of manifestations.

Foremost, it was crafted to possess an inherent sense of curiosity and restlessness. It became bored easily.

Due to its vastness, Breath possessed the ability to divide into distinct gases that subsequently merged to yield water. The aqueous element extended extensively across the terrestrial expanse. This rendered the situation more intriguing; however, the engrossment was short-lived.

Respiration caused the water to carry fragments of the rock into the vast expanses of the oceans. The water exhibited a combination of minerals and salts. After all necessary preparations were made, Breathe immersed itself into the depths of the ocean, effectively assimilating with the mud. Life was begun.

Over the years, the breath of life progressively fostered the growth of various forms and dimensions. It resided within the lushness of woodlands and tropical ecosystems, engaging in the vital process of generating additional oxygen to support the health of our planet.

It resided within the fauna inhabiting the planetary ecosystem, leading to a proliferation of animal species on par with the botanical richness.

One of the creatures present was a human being, who led a simple and humble existence. However, one fateful day, this individual stumbled upon the comforting embrace of fire. He could utilize controlled combustion to generate heat and facilitate the preparation of sustenance by incinerating a fraction of the flora. Similar to plants and animals, fire also requires oxygen to sustain itself.

Over time, humanity discovered its increasingly proficient utilization of botanical, faunal, and mineral resources to enhance its quality of life, albeit occasionally engaging in conflicts over the acquisition of said resources from fellow individuals.

Consequently, this persisted until the inhalation of breath was impeded by the noxious smoke and vapors emitted as men incessantly pursued the creation of luxuries. The coughing generated strong winds and cyclones. The respiration process was being utilized, potentially maltreated, and it was deeply contemplating departing from this celestial body in search of another habitat where its value would be duly recognized. Following all of Breath's creations, humanity was currently dismantling its accomplishments.

The remaining fauna were perishing, flora were being deprived of sustenance and suffocated, and the natural resources were being depleted to support what was deemed opulence, as well as to manufacture destructive arms that would accelerate the demise of all living beings.

This phenomenon ultimately encapsulated the essence of what was colloquially referred to as civilization, as it concurrently brought about profound adversity for the less privileged individuals inhabiting the globe. Only a minor percentage of the human population is able to reside in a state of comfort.

Due to the entirety of the circumstances, Breath came up with a strategy. It would result in the departure of the planet, leaving behind a desolate and unproductive mass of inert matter.

Subsequently, it would resume its cycle, albeit with the notable absence of humanity.

## Case Studies

Inquiry from my client - Case study 1

The perspective of this individual starkly contrasts, as he expressed, "In my interactions with my spouse, I am often met with dismissive remarks such as 'oh shut up,' whereas disregarding her and not giving due attention also elicits complaints from her." What are her expectations? She expresses her preference for me not to cause any disruptions and not to undertake any tasks.

...................................................
...............................................

(My reply)

This narrative bears resemblance to the classic conundrum of the chicken and the egg. Which one came first? Which came first, the chicken or the egg? Nobody knows. It is indicative of a specific aspect within the narrative you are conveying to me. If I were to consult your wife, she would undoubtedly present an alternative perspective. It is essential to acknowledge that the dynamics of a marital relationship are best delineated by the individuals involved. A significant challenge in determining the dynamics of marital relationships involves the delicate task of managing and reconciling the emotional burdens carried within the context of familial responsibilities. I trust you are familiar with the concept of a bank account. Suppose I have accumulated a sum of $1000 in my bank account; it is not possible for me to exceed the withdrawal limit of $1000. This situation bears resemblance to the interpersonal challenge he is encountering. I would categorize this as a "romantic reserve" where withdrawals are impossible without prior deposits. I politely inquired the husband to contemplate whether he is seeking to extract more love from his wife than he has invested in her. He subsequently found the answer.

Psychologists have delineated two distinct cognitive frameworks pertaining to couples – namely, the "traditional thinking style" and the "modern thinking style". Of the two, the traditional thinking style exhibits a tendency to adopt a blame-centric approach by assigning culpability to one another. I would prefer not to engage in conversation with you at this time.

The contemporary mindset revolves around the question of "How can I influence my partner's behavior in a manner that aligns with my expectations for myself and my family?"

Case Study 2

That is the identical set of relationship issues that occurred between an employer and an employee. During a coaching session I conducted with an MNC company, a subordinate approached me to express that his superior consistently acknowledges the achievements of another employee, despite the fact that he surpasses the other employee in terms of productivity, yet fails to receive the necessary recognition from his boss. Subsequently, I inquired of him, "What, in your opinion, is the rationale behind the boss's appreciation of this specific colleague?"

I instructed him to compile a list of four tasks or activities that his colleague is engaged in, in order for his superior to acknowledge his efforts. After enumerating these four items, I inquired if he could undertake a parallel task for his superior. Subsequently, he informed me of his inability to undertake the task, prompting me to assert that he lacks the authority to become agitated.

He alluded to another issue pertaining to the strained dynamics within his marital relationship.

I provided him with knowledge about NLP (neuro linguistic psychology) therapy in the context of family dynamics. Based on the principles of NLP , society can be categorized into three distinct personality types known as

Individuals with VAK inclinations, encompassing visual, auditory, and kinesthetic preferences.

If you possess a visual inclination, your mindset revolves around the belief that "seeing is believing." For individuals who possess an auditory learning style, their cognitive inclination can be described as "Valuing what is heard is synonymous with belief." If you possess a strong inclination towards emotions, specifically the belief that one's feelings are a determinant of their beliefs, may it be inferred that you have designated yourself as a V.A or a K.?

By recognizing the presence of this particular disposition within both you and your spouse, it is possible to diminish the divide in your relationship. You possess a solution for that. If one possesses a preference for visual stimuli, their manner of communication with their spouse will consistently entail the use of visual elements. If she does not possess a visual inclination, her reactions will consistently manifest in a non-visual manner. The majority of the case studies presented to our clinic exhibit similar characteristics.

Case study 3

Let us examine the dynamics of a romantic partnership through the lens of

Neuro-Linguistic Programming (NLP) philosophy. The husband possesses a predilection for visual stimuli. On the occasion of their 10th wedding anniversary, he has purchased for her an exquisitely designed, red gown from a renowned fashion house, as he firmly believed in the sentiment, "What I appreciate resonates with her as well." These vibrant offerings symbolize his affectionate gesture. Furthermore, he presented her with a bouquet of roses, as he values their grandeur, vibrant hues, and believes that she will derive similar joy from them. Therefore, he discreetly departs during the nocturnal hours of his 10th anniversary to present his wife with the aforementioned gift. However, it is worth noting that his wife possesses a predilection for sensory experiences rather than visual stimuli - she is inclined towards tactile sensations, epitomizing a kinesthetic nature. She accepted it quietly and returned it. This individual was contemplating the reason behind his wife's unresponsive behavior, as it did not align with his expectations. After a span of several days, he assumed a significantly more solemn demeanor. He proceeded to inquire of his spouse as to why she did not exhibit a similar level of love and affection that he bestowed upon her during the evening of their 10th anniversary. I have invested a substantial amount, exceeding $3000, to ensure your aesthetic appeal by procuring a vibrant sari and several accompanying gifts. However, it appears that you have chosen to retain these items without expressing any gratitude or acknowledgement. Might you be able to surmise the response of the lady?

The woman expressed, (in relation to my profession) "I do not desire your beautiful sari; I would derive greater satisfaction if you were to temporarily abstain from your duties in order to spend quality time in my company." I would have experienced greater contentment. "From which paradigm is she speaking; she embodies a kinesthetic disposition, characterized by her strong sensitivity towards emotions. You grasp the essence." Yep. Thus, her method of communication is predominantly based on emotions, while the gentleman's approach relies heavily on visual imagery.

There appears to be no inherent issue, however, two alternative courses of action are available to address this matter. Either the husband must reconcile himself with the kinesthetic preferences of his wife, or alternatively, the wife should seek to grasp the visual inclinations of her husband. . You demonstrate characteristics consistent with the Visual, Auditory, and Kinesthetic learning styles. Once you have identified the discrepancy, you can proceed to ascertain strategies aimed at reducing the disparity.

It is imperative for individuals to possess a comprehensive understanding of one another.

NLP for Salesman.

Typically, this occurrence transpires when a patron enters the textile showroom and subsequently queues up. This customer appears to have a delicate constitution and is in search of drapery that offers a variety of colors and patterns to examine. However, as a shop proprietor with a vested interest in attracting his patronage, he presumes that nearly all individuals who enter the establishment will be captivated by its aesthetic appeal. He proceeded to display a selection of aesthetically pleasing shirts that were unsuitable for the tropical climate, resulting in a mismatch in terms of appropriateness. Upon witnessing this event, the female sales manager recommended to the sales boy that he should ensure the customer feels at ease. He heeded the counsel and expressed to the gentleman, "Should you acquire this garment, you will hardly perceive its presence due to its exceptional lightness." Subsequently, the connection was established, leading to a natural and effortless conversation between both parties. (The customer exhibited a preference for kinesthetic learning)

What the audience wants

What inquiries pertain to the interests of the audience? What are the essential messages that should be conveyed by every presentation, regardless of the subject or material?

Are there any latent inquiries that the spectators must have resolved prior to engaging in attentive listening? You know there are. These are identical queries that were posed by you at the inception of this workshop.

As you commence your presentation, the individuals in the audience are harboring these inquiries within their thoughts. It is likely that they lack conscious awareness of these questions; nevertheless, they still require resolution.

They are questions like:

Do we share any similarities?

Do I like you?

Do I trust you?

Do I believe you?

Do you believe you?

Are you knowledgeable about the subject matter being discussed?

Does this pertain to my specific circumstances?

Do I respect you?

Additional inquiries could arise, contingent upon the circumstances.

What are the indicators of one's preference for an individual? Is it due to the assertion that "You are able to form a favorable opinion of me" or is there another reason for this perception?

It would be advantageous to contemplate the overarching message that permeates your presentations, placing it at the forefront of your planning process. If you establish that as a premise, all subsequent actions will have a robust basis for development.

It is highly advisable to allocate time for this purpose, as allowing the audience to discover the answers to these inquiries will guarantee their undivided attention at a later stage.

Environment

Please be aware that the context in which you deliver your presentation will significantly impact the audience's perception and the overall success of your objectives, especially if you carefully orchestrate the environment to align with the audience's anticipated experience.

Consider not only the location and facility, but also the aspects of branding and signage that contribute to the audience's expectations.

Additionally, considerations such as providing refreshments and utilizing a lectern could be taken into account. By assuming a position behind a lectern, you risk diminishing your rapport with the audience, as it obstructs their visual connection with you. In the event that water is accessible to you, it can serve as a means to grant yourself a period of reflection for pondering inquiries.

The natural milieu has the capacity to either facilitate or impede your progress towards attaining your desired objective. Therefore, it would be prudent to allocate a portion of your attention towards contemplating this aspect.

Structuring the presentation

Please be mindful that achievement, within the context of natural language processing, does not involve simply contemplating on what might be effective and disregarding potential non-effective options. Instead, it entails diligently examining and observing the outcomes of various approaches to determine their efficacy.

Framing

By providing instructions or directives to individuals, you assist them in discerning and prioritizing relevant information that is beneficial to them. If instructions are not provided until the conclusion, individuals will be entirely ill-equipped and unlikely to comply with your request. This procedure is commonly referred to as labelling or framing, and it is frequently employed instinctively by individuals possessing adept communication skills.

I intend to deliver certain information, following which I would appreciate your valuable input.

I will be delivering a comprehensive update on the project, following which I kindly request your valuable feedback.

I intend to submit a proposal for your consideration, subsequent to which I kindly request your decision.

Outcome focus

A commonly cited maxim among seasoned instructors of presentation techniques is to employ a three-step approach: commence by providing an overview of your upcoming content, subsequently elaborate on the subject matter, and finally recapitulate the key points conveyed throughout the presentation. Put simply, the audience possesses a finite capacity for attention, thus necessitating the need to effectively impart your message. Here's an updated version:

Please communicate your desired actions to them.

Provide the necessary information for them to accomplish the task.

Communicate to them the specific tasks or actions you wish for them to undertake.

Association (shifting referential index)

Commence by discussing the broader context and individuals collectively, subsequently transitioning towards a more pertinent subset of the populace, followed by focusing on the individuals present in the immediate environment, progressing towards addressing the second person, and eventually incorporating the first person perspective. "The referential index undergoes a transition in the following manner:

The hierarchical order of individuals can be described as follows: everyone (or everything) is of greater importance than them, us ranks higher than you, and I is of the least significance in comparison.

Timeframe – commonly referred to as 'overall retrospective tempo'

Initiate from a antecedent period, enumerating all the collective encounters leading up to the current juncture, with the aim of establishing a mutual state of accord, subsequently progressing chronologically to ensue determination towards a prospective course of action.

Frame/story/question

Structure the communication in a manner that effectively captures the audience's interest, through framing, narrating a concise anecdote, and posing a thought-provoking question in order to redirect their mindset and reorient their attention.

Pacing current experience

The initial objective you must accomplish in your presentation is to captivate the attention of the audience. One can inquire, impart personal information, utilize an introductory statement, share a humorous anecdote, or employ any other appropriate approach within the given circumstances.

A highly effective approach to attaining this objective is to cultivate an audience predisposed to an "agreement state," wherein they are inclined to align with your standpoint, regard your ideas positively, and ultimately make the desired choices.

At present, you are perusing these written words and contemplating your upcoming presentation. It is conceivable that you have previously engaged in presentations, or have been the recipient of presentations by others. In either scenario, you might possess the inclination to strive for excellence and enhance the proficiency in your existing pursuits. It is commendable that you are demonstrating such a proactive commitment to self-improvement, as you are well aware of the positive outcomes it will yield for you.

Could you identify any points of contention within the preceding paragraph? Was there any point of concurrence?

In the initial section, we discussed the action of regulating the mental and emotional state of the audience. This process remains unchanged, but now you will be closely attending to their experience. As you commence by presenting universally applicable information, you will observe the audience exhibiting concurrence through affirmative gestures. As your presentation grows more focused and moves away from the realm of pure facts, it is highly probable that they will find themselves more inclined toward agreement rather than disagreement. To illustrate, it is accurate to assert that you are engaging in the study of presentation skills. It is a contention to assert that reading is the most effective means of developing one's presentation skills. Your convictions - the advantages of your product, opinions, or proposals - are apt to receive greater acceptance if your audience is in a state of agreement. During the application of hypnosis, we employ a straightforward set of instructions that guides the individual through alternating periods of engaging with their immediate surroundings and directing their attention inward:

Please communicate three observations to your partner that you are aware they can perceive through their senses.

Kindly inform your partner of one potential truth - a proposition

Inquire with your partner regarding their level of awareness.

Recite on four or five occasions.
What is the rationale behind including a discussion on hypnosis in a section dedicated to the art of delivering presentations? Now, let us consider the scenario within the framework of a formal presentation.

Please elucidate three current verities or commonly shared encounters to the audience.

Kindly proffer a notion to the spectators that could potentially be veracious - a proposition.

Solicit the consensus of the audience
And you may still be curious as to how this relates to the act of presenting. Thus, I shall offer a few illustrations, commencing with a recurring remark often encountered at sales conferences.
This year has presented considerable challenges

Competition has been intense
We've worked hard
Your objectives are set to increase twofold in the coming year.
Effective leadership plays a pivotal role in achieving business prosperity.
Effective leaders motivate their employees.
Leadership can be derived from innate qualities or cultivated through nurture.
Peter Freeth enhances and cultivates your capacity for effective leadership.
It is consistently beneficial to ensure that your audience is receptive before commencing the transmission of information. This straightforward method is an immensely influential approach to guiding the audience towards a receptive state by imparting to them veracious information - encompassing either their personal encounters or the current era, as an illustration:
Each and every one of you has made the journey to be present on this occasion.
We are all together
You can hear me

Please feel free to take a moment to find a comfortable position.

We have a few presentations scheduled prior to the lunch break.

A number of you may be inquisitive.

It is possible that some of you are already aware.

I am aware that you might have inquiries

You may be questioning, "how shall I proceed with this?"

And undoubtedly, when the audience is in a receptive disposition, they are more prone to concur with your perspective.

www.ingramcontent.com/pod-product-compliance
Lightning Source LLC
Chambersburg PA
CBHW050418120526
44590CB00015B/2013